# THE SECRET LECTURER

**Secret Lecturer**

T0333607

*First published by Canbury Press 2024*
*This edition published 2024*

*Canbury Press*
*Kingston upon Thames, Surrey, United Kingdom*
*www.canburypress.com*

*Printed and bound in Great Britain*
*Typeset in Athelas (body), Futura PT (heading)*

*This is a work of non-fiction*

*FSC® helps take care of forests for future generations.*

*ISBN:*
*Paperback 9781914487217*
*Ebook 9781914487224*

# THE SECRET LECTURER

## What Really Goes on at University

### Secret Lecturer

# Contents

# Introduction

For many people the question, 'Are British universities f***ed?' is as rhetorical as 'Does the Supreme Pontiff devoutly believe in the monotheistic faith he leads?' or 'Do members of the *Ursidae* family of carnivoran mammals defecate in arboreal regions?' But people weren't saying this 30 years ago. Why not? What's happened to British universities?

When it comes to higher education (HE), everyone has an opinion, whether they know anything about it or not. This may be down to its extraordinary growth in recent decades and its high profile in the media today. If you haven't been to university yourself, you might know one or more of the 800,000 people they employ – or some of the 9.1 million people studying in one. In the 1950s, only three percent of the UK population went to university, whereas now the figure is closer to 40 percent. HE is today worth £95 billion a year to the British economy and has re-shaped the demographics, built environments and economies of entire towns and cities across the country.

But this narrative is not one of pure progress. According to a survey in 2023, 42 percent of current students do not think their studies represent value for money. The harshest criticisms of HE come from those outside it. Policymakers and politicians such as Suella Braverman and Jacob Rees-Mogg, as well as large elements of the public and mass-media, deride some university courses for being 'Mickey Mouse' and an arrant waste of time and money. They say that academic standards are slipping, that both students and academics are lazy and that HE has been paralysed by bureaucracy and managerialism. Those on the right of the political spectrum – and indeed some in the centre – are convinced that all these problems boil down to the 'woke' seizure of universities by 'snowflakes' who have abandoned serious intellectual enquiry for far-left politics and an obsession with 'de-platforming' those with whom they disagree.

As one who for the last 15 years has lectured at a British university in various arts and humanities subjects, I can say that most – but not all – of these slurs are incorrect. It's high time someone who at least partly knows what they are talking about set the record straight.

As you will see from these diaries, the biggest fib is the one about wokeness. Spend a fraction of time inside a university in the United Kingdom and you'll rapidly discover they are ruthless corporations that were recently declared 'institutionally racist' by Prof David Richardson, chair of Universities UK's advisory group on racism. They're sexist, homophobic and transphobic, too, according to the multitude of bullying cases I've heard about, not to say the microaggressions I've witnessed. It's quite something when the chair of a university multicultural society is forced to step down because they have been victims of racism and sexism. And I don't know about you, but nothing screams 'Watch out for those pinko tofu-snorting PC apparatchiks!' quite like doing millions of pounds' worth of business with arms dealers, fossil fuel companies and foreign dictatorships – or swiftly promoting colleagues who deny climate change and defend extra-judicial killing. We've moved a long way from the liberal ideal of the academic as an independent critic of power and privilege. To add insult to injury, university leaders try to cloak such nastiness in the rhetoric of 'equality', 'diversity', 'human rights' and 'decolonisation'. This, I am sure, is every consolation to a Yemeni or Palestinian who's just lost half their family to a British-made rocket.

On a more trivial level, the UK public seem to think a university lecturer is an idle, sherry-swigging stereotype out of a 1970s campus novel. Perceptions of students are frozen in the 1980s – they're either idle, undernourished wimps à la Neil from the BBC sitcom *The Young Ones* or like his housemates Rick (naïvely militant blowhard) or Vyvyan (shouty, intoxicated hooligan). Many of the students I teach are well-behaved, eat healthily and aren't uniformly obsessed with getting smashed. Some of them even vote Conservative. But an even more disturbing development that few in the '80s could have predicted is the epidemic of mental illness among students – and staff. Readers may be surprised to find out that legions of lecturers are overworked and underpaid, and on casual contracts.

As you will also see, academic standards are slowly being obliterated, though that has more to do with financing than with a slide into 'wokery'. The conversion of students into customers we can't afford to upset has resulted in an upsurge in grades, non-attendance, abusive behaviour and plagiarism. Hardly anyone ever fails no matter how badly they perform. Not to be left out, lecturers can plagiarise, too – usually each other's lecture notes and research ideas. A mania about external funding has destroyed research ethics.

The effective privatisation of universities that began under New Labour in the late '90s and has been steroid-driven under the Tories since 2010, was supposed to magically transform universities from flabby, wasteful public sloths into sleek, dynamic, private cheetahs. The truth is that the modern university is the worst of both species. As Peter Fleming in his unsettling book *Dark Academia* (2021) puts it: 'The 1997 Dearing Report and then the Browne Review in 2010 basically privatised government spending via the student loans system… and universities [had to] compete for business. This artificial market merely transformed universities into desperate cash-hunting machines.'

From my perspective on the ground, I watch classrooms crumble, departments close and able colleagues being made redundant due to 'lack of funding.' Meanwhile, fortunes are wasted on dodgy investments and perilously incompetent senior managers. When staff plan to strike, they're threatened with the sack and morally blackmailed about 'causing poor student feedback.'

If all this sounds too depressing, some positives remain. Despite all the slings and arrows raining down on them, many of my students remain curious, creative, thoughtful and socially aware. At the end of this book, I even make some humble proposals for improving HE. Not that anyone will listen to them…

While the incidents recounted below are fundamentally true, in real life they took place over a longer period than the 'academic year' that this book spans. I've used this format because, to be frank, I hope it'll make for a better read. I've also changed small details about these episodes such as using initials to refer to other people. There are several vitally important reasons for this. Firstly, I want to protect the privacy of colleagues and students I care about – and even the ones I don't. Despite being a British academic in the 2020s, I do have a moral compass. Moreover, I can't have people sussing out who I am because I can't afford to lose my job... unless the book you're holding becomes a bestseller, which it almost certainly won't.

# Semester 1

# September 15th

With a few days before teaching begins, my colleague E and I try to finish writing a conference paper we're due to give next month. We can't do this in our office because it's open-plan and noisy. The three cupboard-sized tutorial rooms next door are booked all day. To put this into perspective, 40 lecturers and about 400 students are expected to use only these three rooms. The building was recently refurbished for £6.1 million – but apparently that didn't include creating spaces in which to work.

We check several empty classrooms. They've all been locked since the pandemic. Nobody knows why. We try to book an alternative with our receptionist. By this point, we'd settle for an unclean toilet cubicle.

Only a giant lecture theatre is free. We go in, place our laptops on a lectern and work standing up. Five minutes later, a caretaker enters with an electric drill. 'Sorry, lads, you might want to pop out – gonna be noisy for an hour.'

# September 17th

I meet two new adjunct lecturers who have been allocated a grand total of ten hours' teaching each this semester. Such is HE's passion for cost-cutting, 70% of all lecturers in the UK have the same status. I give them documents relating to the units they are covering and recall that no one did me such a favour when I started as an adjunct a decade and a half ago. My first few weeks were thus terrifying. When I mentioned my quandary to an older, full-time colleague, he patted me on the back and said, 'I don't know what you're doing, they [management] don't know what you're doing, and you don't know what you're doing. But whatever it is you *are* doing, it's probably fine.' I found that strangely reassuring.

Being isolated has its plus points. Whereas our counterparts in schools are under constant surveillance by government inspectors, we're left alone as long as we don't get terrible student feedback. My superiors have never asked me a single question about the content, structure or methods of my teaching. Sometimes I wish they would ask, as some classes go quite well and I'd like my bosses to know. Thus, I've devised entire units from scratch based on my own research and industry experience. The complete absence of support means I have had to trust my own instincts that I'm doing the right thing.

# September 18th

First day of teaching. A small third-year class. They're all small nowadays. My record achieved last year is two seminars in a row with zero attendance. It's hard not to take it personally. It's also baffling to me that students are paying over £9,000 a year to *not* turn up to anything.

We're interrupted just before the end by A, an Australian-origin student, pressing his orange face against the window of the door. His hip-slung keyring and cargo trousers remind me of a skater punk from my own student days. I try to ignore him. But when the entire class begins staring at him standing there, staring at us, I must act. 'So, A, are you coming in?'

He opens the door, hyperventilating. He pauses halfway to one of the myriad empty chairs. 'Ah... ah, actually, I'll come see you after class. Aight?'

He comes back in after the others have left, still blushing but not hyperventilating. He won't remove his fingerless-gloved hand from his mouth.

'Are you alright, A?'

'Man... man... man....'

'Are you feeling unwell?'

'Yeah. Spaced out. Spaced out.'

I ask: 'Has something bad happened?' I regret asking – I'm not a trained counsellor. Then again, I'm contractually obliged to offer 'pastoral care' to students. That's one of many contradictions in this job. I decide that just asking a few questions can't be that bad. This situation can hardly get much worse.

A nods rapidly, like a piston. 'Yeah, bad. Bad. Bad.'

'Why don't you take a seat?'

He does so and crosses his legs tightly, glove still locked to face.

'Want some water?' I spot leftover mineral water bottles and plastic cups from an event that took place before my class.

'Naah, I'm good. Sorry about this, I'm just ah... under a lotta... under a lotta stress.'

'Don't have to be sorry.'

'I'm struggling, man. Struggling... The assessment... Shit.'

'Well we can talk about that now, if you like. Or whenever you're ready to.'

'Sorry. I'm so *so* sorry.'

'It's fine. Really.'

'I mean... I'm not sorry about *that*. Oh, shit....'

'What are you sorry about?'

He looks away guiltily.

'How did you travel here today, A?'

'The bus.'

'Did something happen on the bus to upset you?'

'You know when, like....' He breaks off.

'Shall I call student wellbeing?'

'Ahh…'

'I think it's best, A. You seem like you need help and I'm not at all qualified to give it.' I phone wellbeing and find out from a chatty, upbeat woman that there's a three-month waiting list for student appointments. 'Can you have a quick word with A now?' I ask. No, she's just a manager. I hang up.

'If we can talk,' A says, 'man to man....'

'I guess so.' I'm now feeling almost as anxious as him.

'You know when you, like, come? When a guy comes?'

'Yes, I am aware of… that.' The absolute last thing I want to do is talk to a student about sex.

Another student, a very able and perceptive one who graduated a few years ago, complained to me about a colleague who had waxed at length about love scenes in soap operas. 'I really don't want a 50-year-old man in a Batman T-shirt talking to me about shagging,' she said. I could see her point.

'And after you come, you go to the restroom,' continues C, 'and, like, when you pee, it kinda divides into two streams. And it's... it's kinda annoying 'cause one of the streams goes in the bowl and the other goes on the floor.'

I don't know what to say.

'Well, oh man... the bus....' He laughs maniacally. 'The fuckin' bus.'

'Are you saying that you.... You don't have to answer that.'

He looks at me, brow deepening, eyes foggy.

'A, if this isn't a personal question, do you smoke weed? Whatever you tell me will be in confidence.'

He takes his hand away from his mouth. 'Uh-huh.'

'Did you smoke some weed before you got on the bus?'

'I'm always blazin'. Do you smoke weed?'

'Only a couple of times. Many years ago.'

'Why... why d'you only have it a couple of times?'

'It made me paranoid. Look, A, do you live with your family?'

'My mom.'

I reach for the phone. 'Shall I call her to come and pick you up?'

'No, don't... don't do that.'

'What about a friend then?'

'I could call T at work. She'll be finishing her shift soon.'

'Could she meet you at the bus stop?'

'Yeah, I think... I think.'

'Okay then, take care, A, and email me to let me know you got home alright.'

I open the door for him. He stays in the seat, looking close to tears again. Is he psyching himself up? How long is it reasonable to wait for him to do that? Would some further chit-chat chill him out?

After about 30 seconds, I say: 'A, are you going to walk to the bus stop now? I don't think we can stay here all night.'

'Man….' He starts hyperventilating again.

'Do you want me to come – walk – with you?'

'Yeah… that'd be nice. Thanks, man.'

I do as required. As the bus arrives, A extends a gloved hand. I pat him on the shoulder instead. Once there is some distance between us, I give him a wave.

On the walk back from the bus stop, I speculate on the causes of A's woes. Where to start? Obviously, there are problems at home. One doesn't need to be Dr Freud to assume he feels ignored or under-loved by his mum. I get the sense also that his generation experiences life as a buffet of artificial realities. When there's the constant temptation to alter your state of mind with booze, weed, pharmaceutical mood-boosters, social media and computer games, might you confuse the boundaries? Maybe, momentarily, when he did whatever he did on the bus, he thought it wouldn't have material consequences, just as shooting down a helicopter in *Far Cry 6* doesn't.

Our university must take some responsibility too. As I swipe my card to enter our open-plan office, a Ford Focus is paused on the double yellow lines, its stereo playing 'We are Family' by Sister Sledge. The lyrical sentiment couldn't be further removed from the modern student experience. Lost souls like A are alienated from day one. They're treated impersonally as customers, yet not as valued ones – the jaded lecturers, long waiting lists for services, extortionate halls of residence and sub-optimal workspaces attest to that. Students are paying all this money but are not given any stake in or say over how their university is run. The oppressively sterile design of the campus can't be good for the soul either. Our foyer is bristling with security cameras, staffed by beaming women in suits and scarves, and you can't get 20 feet around the building without having to produce your ID card. It's somewhere between a military base, international airport and high street bank branch. Is it any wonder, then, that kids don't feel like they belong here, that they are emphatically *not* part of any family?

# September 19th

A man whose job it is to provide chairs visits me in the morning. Sitting in my current chair has become about as comfortable as caressing an electric fence. I have perpetual neck and back ache. Chair Man brings with him an extraordinary steampunkish contraption rippling with levers, gears, knobs and pulleys. 'Try this out for size,' he says.

It feels a lot better.

He spends half an hour demonstrating the chair's myriad functions. I get embarrassed as I realise that others in the open-plan office can't see what he's doing but *can* hear him say things like, 'Reach down and have a fiddle around with this' and 'If I pull the knob this way, does it feel good?'

# September 20th

First-year lecture. Slightly more students present since this is a compulsory unit. To get the students thinking about the essay they must write about their creative influences, I ask each one to mention a favourite artist or author – and why.

'Grayson Perry,' says one. 'He's funny.'

I write that on the whiteboard.

'B.S. Johnson,' says another. 'I like his nonlinear sort of shit.'

I write most of that on the whiteboard, but not 'sort of shit.'

'Tony Parsons,' says the next student. 'I think he's right about a lot of, like, political stuff.'

I don't write that down, but I do remember showing them a thinkpiece Parsons had penned for the *Sun* during a World Cup. It was a list of English things that he loved... to express his passion for the England team, presumably. Among the duff lines was, '[I love] George Orwell and George Michael.'

To my sorrow, the entire class loved it. Now one of the students is citing Parsons as a major influence.

# September 22nd

The polar opposite of yesterday's class. This seminar group of third-years are friendlier to me and each other. They're more ethnically diverse and intellectually curious. Most remarkably, they actually read stuff.

However, our location takes the shine off. Due to the odd decision to lock up so many classrooms, I'm now doing more of my teaching in small spaces in the university library. While the class discussion is rich and rewarding, we're all distracted by the damp stains spilling across the rear wall and the three buckets on the carpet. It's been raining heavily and there's a leak. Which nobody has fixed.

# September 23rd

Department meeting. Ninety-nine per cent of these are pointless, their topics easily dealt with by email. But our Head of Department (HoD) instigated them to make it look like he was busy. I don't know what he does apart from this, but he's been doing not much for so long that he now earns more than a professor, many of whom don't do much either.

My HoD misspeaks so egregiously that he should join the hallowed ranks of George W. Bush and Joe Biden. He says, 'Most of us here aren't research active. Those of you who do research – well, it's the sort of thing that you'd do for fun, on evenings and weekends, isn't it?' Not only has he managed to offend a third of the people in the room, but he's let slip that he doesn't have a clue about how exacting it is to write a book or journal article, curate an exhibition, make a film or compose a symphony. Moreover, if you take research out of universities, you're left with nothing to distinguish them from schools and FE colleges.

In the evening, I drink too much and browse YouTube. I find a recording of a smarmy, well-built bloke – whom I'll call Prof X – talking about self-promotion. He stands beside his PowerPoint presentation for a moment, beaming.

'Did somebody say something?' he begins. Nobody in the audience did, so everyone looks puzzled. 'Oh sorry,' says Prof X. 'Must be the voices inside my head.'

In a climate where huge numbers of staff and students are suffering from depression, anxiety and a host of other mental illnesses, this is not a vastly appropriate comment.

'But I'm not joking,' says Prof X. 'I've been diagnosed with PTSD.' He goes on to tell us that his research field is the stress endured by those servicepeople who operate 'new military technologies.' Not once does he mention the people who get blown to smithereens by that same tech. Startlingly, he tries to mount a moral defence of these methods as the 'most humane' way to wage the 'War on Terror.' He does not appear to consider that such methods have been widely condemned by legal experts as extrajudicial killing. Aside from that, his research isn't rigorous. *White people in Aldershot fiddle with joysticks and slaughter brown people in Somalia. These white people get depressed about it. And that's it.* None of these propositions amount to a contestable thesis. One would hope for more from a professor.

Prof X's last word on the matter is, 'You've really got to *push* yourself out there. If you don't do it, nobody else will.'

# September 24th

Because I am a sad man in a dark place with not much else to do today, I research Prof X. To me, he embodies absolutely everything wrong with the modern university. I find that he has obtained a lot of funding from the arms industry – hence the love of blowing stuff up. He's also done consultancy work for parliament. I thought academics weren't supposed to hobnob with the powerful and parrot their worldview. I thought we were supposed to, as the great Palestinian intellectual Edward Said wrote, 'raise embarrassing questions, confront orthodoxy and dogma (rather than to produce them)' and 'to be someone who cannot easily be co-opted by governments or corporations.'

Well, Prof X has been co-opted. What's changed in HE – UK HE, at least – since Said wrote those words is that it's all about the money now. Since the introduction of student fees in 1998, the end of EU revenue post-Brexit and the Conservatives' halving of public funding for university arts subjects, academics have, like sordid hustlers, been forced onto the streets to solicit partners for cash. There is next to no ethical oversight of this process, so universities merrily join hands with firms that flog weapons to foreign dictatorships and/or are hastening the end of the world by buying, selling or processing fossil fuels. We can add to this list 'university involvement in developing artificial intelligence (AI) surveillance for authoritarian regimes, animal-testing collaborations with private labs and joint projects with big tobacco companies,' as Peter Fleming puts it in his erudite diagnosis of almost everything wrong with the modern academy.

And there are double standards galore – whereas in 2011, the director of the LSE resigned after it transpired that Colonel Gadaffi and his son had donated £1.5 million to that institution, I can't see any VC quitting over *Open Democracy*'s recent revelations about £7 million of Russian oligarchs' money sloshing about in their coffers. On the contrary, those knee-deep in my uni's mucky trysts with Turkey and Saudi Arabia are more likely to spring straight to the top of the academic ladder.

While I'm Googling Prof X, I stumble upon a *Daily Mail* article headlined 'The woke brigade have hijacked academia.'

This is a typical right-wing view, but if Paul Dacre or Suella Braverman were to pop into my university, they'd feel right at home amid the arms dealers, climate change denialists and theocratic fascists.

# September 25th

I spend the day organising a public-facing event. This is the kind of thing the top brass want us to do for 'community outreach.' I do it because I enjoy it. Most of my colleagues can't be bothered.

I get into an email dispute with our building manager, who is on the same pay as a professor. The building closes at 5pm sharp whereas I want the event to begin at 6pm, so there will be a chance of people attending it. I ask if a porter can be on hand, since the regular receptionists will have gone home by then. The manager is determined to make this procedure as difficult as planning and executing D-Day.

`There will be extra costs associated with late opening,` the manager writes. `And you'll need to undertake a full risk assessment.`

I ponder what new hazards using a lecture theatre after 5pm poses. Once the sun goes down are people likely to start decapitating themselves with overhead projectors? Will vampires swoop in from Transylvania and mutilate everyone?

Eight emails later, I establish what these extra costs are. £43. To avoid further officiousness, I'm minded to go to the cashpoint, take out the money from my personal account and slam it down on the manager's desk. But that would probably breach protocol.

# September 26th

I come into the office to find colleagues in a mood between bemusement and panic. A tabloid paper has published an 'exposé' of 'Mickey Mouse' courses offered at 'universities gone PC-mad.' Our institution has been named and shamed for 'Critical Meat Raffle Studies.' In a radio phone-in later that morning, some outraged taxpayer has bellowed about kids wasting 'our' money on studying the peculiar British tradition of drunk people winning raw sausages in pubs.

Our HoD is moved to both email the newspaper and call the radio show to explain that 'Critical Meat Raffle Studies' is not an actual functioning unit. It's a made-up test unit that we use to train admin staff in how to manage functioning units. The good reason for the ridiculous title was so that people wouldn't confuse it with something *real*.

# September 28th

I'm puzzled to see on social media a retired female colleague announcing she's editing an anthology of pro-trans-rights essays. I could have sworn that, at a function two months ago, she said to me that transwomen 'are not really women, are they?' Which reminds me of another colleague who made disparaging remarks in a press interview about Jeremy Corbyn in the run-up to the 2017 election. A few days later, when the opinion polls started to show Labour gaining late ground on the Tories, he asked for the article to be updated with a more positive quote.

As an undergrad student some time ago, I remember reading a 17th-century folk song called 'The Vicar of Bray' about a clergyman whose allegiances shift 180 degrees as religious and political paradigms shift:

> *When George in Pudding time came o'er,*
> *And Moderate Men looked big, Sir,*
> *My Principles I chang'd once more,*
> *And so became a Whig, Sir.*

Many of the academics I know are latter-day Vicars of Bray – or Groucho Marxes, for if the company they are in at any one time doesn't like their principles, they'll change theirs. Rather than leading thought, they genuflect to the prevailing intellectual and ideological winds. In that sense, they are like the slickest of politicians. Or just politicians.

Such wavering has kooky limits, though. In the afternoon, I write an email to our research council mildly kvetching about our newsletter celebrating yet another partnership with an arms dealer. Twenty minutes later a professor in our institution responds to me – I wasn't expecting that. He says that he too is very concerned about the influence of the arms industry on HE. What? He takes the arms industry's money for his own research projects.

# September 29th

At 7pm I go to the door of the room that I've booked for the public-facing event I've arranged. It's unlikely anyone will come to it, but I'm an optimist. When I start to open the door, I hear a weird wailing sound like a high wind in a horror film. I close it, alarmed. I'm not paranormally inclined, but if I were, I'd declare the place haunted. What rational explanation could there be? The room's been double-booked for a video-nasty showing? If so, should I go in there and tell them they have half an hour before anyone (any one?) starts arriving for my do? No, that wouldn't be very collegiate.

I go to reception and ask the evening porter to check the room-booking system. 'It's only your event down for 6.30,' he says. 'Looks like earlier we had—' He screws up his eyes at the screen. 'Dunno how to pronounce that....'

'Gamelan music recital,' I say. 'Quite multicultural for this dump.'

'Give 'em a nudge – they should have slung their hooks by four,' says the caretaker.

I can't reconcile the ghostly noise I heard with Indonesian folk music. I go back to the room, start to open the door and hear the wailing again. But once I open the door fully, the noise disappears. The room is vacant. I find out later that the ghostly noise is caused by some interaction between the air-conditioning and the broken rubber seal around the door. That also will never ever be fixed.

# September 30th

Overseas outreach meeting. Two colleagues report on their recent trip to Asia. They unwittingly – or wittingly? – invoke stereotypes. Up flashes a slide of a skyscraper. 'Aww it was just like *Bladerunner* out there!' says someone with a PhD in cultural studies – if not in cultural sensitivity. 'It was boiling hot the whole time,' she says, making a fanning motion with her hand. Next is a picture of a perfectly pleasant-looking young Asian woman. 'Now she *looks* nice,' says my colleague, 'but she was actually, well, a little bit… er… spiky.' It's hard to get my head round the fact that this is a pair of supposedly lefty academics addressing us in the 2020s rather than a pair of Raj civil servants from the 1920s.

# October 2nd

There is a meeting of course heads to discuss last year's results. A fellow head reports that 67% of their students were awarded first-class degrees. 'Nice one,' I laugh. She's deadly serious. I don't know how she can be. I've never taught on a course where more than 10% of the students did that well. I know the students this colleague is talking about – no way are two thirds of them that smart.

# October 4th

I read in our staff bulletin that the course mentioned above has been named the best of its kind in the country… based on the votes of those same students… most of whom received first-class degrees. Any chance whatsoever that such 'grade inflation' – as the more daring of my colleagues are starting to call it – is a wheeze to ensure that students like us lecturers enough to give us positive feedback? Decisions to close departments have been based on such feedback. I dread to think how many lecturers have been fired because they were too honest to bribe students with over-generous marks.

Covid played a poisonous part in all this. A university policy instituted in 2020 acknowledged that students might be underperforming because of lockdown stresses. Some had been marooned in their halls of residence without food. Others had been stranded at their family home sharing a bedroom with a disruptive sibling. There were also bad WiFi connections because parents couldn't afford a better one or lived in the countryside where internet provision is poor. The policy required us to mark the students more generously than usual – on the surface a good idea. But the policy was applied too vigorously, with students who'd done next to nothing – and who hadn't been affected by the lockdowns – walking away with easy firsts and 2.1s.

# October 6th

I hear a raised voice from one of the tutorial cupboards adjacent to our office. I'm a coward so grope for an excuse not to intervene. I'm about to grab my coat and leave when my hand is forced by E storming into the office to ask for help with 'a difficult student.'

The aforesaid little shit is occupying the cupboard. He's commandeered the desktop PC and covered the desk and chairs with his books and papers.

'You can't study in here,' I tell him firmly.

'Where else am I gonna go then? All them rooms up there are locked.'

'The library?'

'Library's too noisy.'

They're right. Our uni library must be the only one in the world where open chatter and even the playing of music is tolerated. I assume this is because we lack the staff to enforce silence.

'There are IT suites in K-Building,' I propose.

'All full up. Look, mate, just leave me alone, alright? I'm studying here. I'm doing what I'm supposed to be doing as a student. You lot should be *grateful* for that.'

I feel a titter coming and manage to cut it off at the back of my throat. 'I can see you're studying hard, it's just you can't do it here. This room is for tutorials and my colleague here has booked it for now.'

'I don't see anyone here but him coming for a tutorial.' The student shrugs.

'That's not the point.'

He looks up at me and scowls. 'You gonna make me leave then?'

'No,' I say. We call security to do that. The sight of a couple of burly bouncer-like guys stomping up the corridor is enough to make him pack his things and skedaddle.

# October 7th

Tutorials in which third-year students tell me about their proposed projects. I'm pleased to see S, an African-Caribbean student who has turned in some insightful work about feeling alienated as a woman of colour in a 'white university in a white town,' as she puts it. She wants to write about the financial strains that students are under. She's calculated the cost of renting a room in one of our privately run new-build halls of residence for a year against how much can be borrowed from the Student Loans Company. According to her, the average loan would only cover the rent until February. The rest – along with food, bills, clothes, etc – must be paid for with a part-time job or by the Bank of Mum and Dad.

'Out of interest, how much is a room in halls?' I ask.

'£170–200 a week,' S replies.

As an undergrad, I recall paying £35 a week. Even taking inflation into account, S and her generation are being royally ripped off.

## October 8th

A minor scandal erupts when our VC is outed by the press as earning £329,000 per annum – 14 times what the lowest-paid employees receive. Students rightly ask what he does for all that – their – money. I don't know. I don't know anyone who knows. I don't think the VC does either.

## October 9th

Staff meeting. The speaker, an academic overseer (AO) – a research-inactive middle manager who's above me but below our HoD – spends the meeting talking about... a load of subsequent meetings due to take place over the rest of the semester. He shows a series of slides with pie charts on them denoting how each future meeting will be divided up time-wise. I'm convinced that everyone in that room – probably including the AO – thinks this is sillier than a stadium full of goats called Billy. No one dares say so, though.

The late philosopher Mark Fisher, who taught in FE, argued that the contemporary British workplace owes a curious debt to Stalin's Russia. Both cultures value 'symbols of achievement over actual achievement' and expend bureaucratic energy on audits, inspections, meetings and other activities that are 'purely symbolic' because 'they will never be acted upon.' It's all about maintaining a façade of efficiency and dynamism, while the reality is anything but. While everyone, Fisher writes, from big swinging dick to piddling skivvy knows the grim reality, the façade remains because it's the 'officially accepted' line pushed by 'PR and propaganda.' This is so true of HE.

# October 3rd

'Well this is fucking boring,' says P, a slightly senior colleague. We're in a Zoom meeting and, yes, he hasn't realised that his microphone is switched on. He has just interrupted a presentation about how the university's overflow car parks operate. I happen to think he's correct.

'Oh, err,' stammers the presenter. 'That's not very nice.'

# October 4th

I bump into a hangdog P at lunchtime. He says that he apologised to the presenter after the meeting. This wasn't good enough for our HoD, who gaslighted him. 'I get the impression you're under a lot of strain,' he said. 'That incident suggests your judgement is lacking. Perhaps you should think about stepping down from your AO role.'

This strikes P as Machiavellian, for only two weeks ago that same HoD had signed off on his glowing performance review. P suspects that another colleague, who is tight with the HoD, is angling for his job and the pair of them are looking for excuses to depose him.

# October 5th

I attend a PhD viva as internal examiner. I wish I wasn't, as the thesis needs serious revision. Not only is it full of misreadings of other scholars but it hasn't been proofread. From almost every page tumble spelling and grammar errors. I have no idea why the student's supervisor ever let her submit it.

In the pre-meeting with the external examiner, I'm relieved that he agrees with me about how sorry the work is. I'm even more relieved when he volunteers to break the news to the student at the end of the viva, because I'm a coward.

The student comes in and the grilling begins. It's heartbreaking – she's so cheery and polite that I feel awful pointing out all her mistakes. At the end when we tell her she needs to make major corrections, she clings onto her smile but she can't stop her eyes glistening.

She's not alone. I know of at least two other doctoral candidates who were told at their vivas to completely rewrite and resubmit their theses. I'm also aware of one who, after submitting, was told by their examiners that it wasn't even worth holding the viva, such was the abysmal quality of their work.

How do we get into this mess? The answer, once again, is financial. These are self-funded students and we're ravenous for their cash. Academic nous is an afterthought. We're exploiting a desire for the social capital derived from being able to call yourself a doctor, to tell your friends and relatives and colleagues that you have a PhD, that you're *that* clever. And that's about all there is to be had from such a qualification given how few academic jobs are out there.

# October 9th

A briefing from our executive dean of faculty. She uses all the grimmest HE newspeak. The word *innovative* now means something that could turn a profit. *Creativity* is bandied about by dullards. Every event, from the smallest convocation about new library holdings to large showcases of research, has to be called a *festival* – as if it will involve crowd-surfing and ecstasy. What used to be dubbed *rooms* or *offices* are now *hubs*. In a gaffe that goes unchallenged, the dean describes the pre-degree period of a new calendar system to be introduced next academic year as 'Year Zero.' How can someone with a history PhD have never heard of Pol Pot?

In the Q&A, colleagues ask reasonable questions. When will the ancient – and possibly hazardous – lights in the basement be updated? Will lecturers be given any more time for research? How do we all improve student attendance?

The replies are feeble. One of the nonsense answers is: 'We'll be cascading that concern upwards.' Mostly, the dean's strategy – which is replicated across management – is to say that 'things are in process' or that 'the conversation about issue A [this works equally well for B, C, and D] is ongoing.' These are the dean's shifty ploys to insulate herself from criticism. These processes never end and it appears to be an unwritten rule that that no tangible action will arise from these meetings. Why make yourself a hostage to fortune, when you can perpetually evaluate *targets* and *aspirations*?

In her last non-answer, the dean starts making a curious winding gesture and wanders into the path of the projector beam so that the university logo appears emblazoned onto her forehead.

# October 10th

I pass a queue of students outside the door of one of the tutorial cupboards. They're grimacing into their phones. I recognise two of them and say hello. 'We're waiting for J,' they tell me. J is one of the laziest academics in the history of the cosmos. He is infamous for missing about half all his classes every year. I don't believe he's ever done a shred of admin – apart from perhaps shredding some incriminating documents. I cannot recall receiving a single email from him in ten years. In marking-meetings, he spends thirty seconds skim-reading submissions before deciding on their grades.

My marking-meetings with J would go something like this. I'd call him at 11am and he'd sound like he was at the pub. I would ask J when he planned to get to campus and he would say 'half an hour.' An hour later, we'd meet in the refectory and compare notes. I'd present him with borderline cases that I needed a second opinion on. He'd snatch one out of my hand, glance at it, hand it back to me and tell me with authority, 'We would normally give that sixty-four rather than seventy-one.' Before I could ask myself, 'How can you possibly decide that in a second when I took twenty minutes and still don't know?' he'd be busy writing a second marker comment so vague that, upon reading it, the student would immediately think their submission hadn't been properly read. And they'd be right. J would then inflict the same damage on a dozen other submissions.

Are there many academics like this? A friend who's quite senior in university administration doubts – with all sincerity – that anyone has ever read a PhD thesis all the way through. I fret about my own qualifications. Were they awarded by roulette too?

To be fair, I've learned over the years that most academics work hard. I've just done a 90-hour week (including evenings and weekends) of admin, teaching preparation and research. But lazy bastards like him dent our collective reputation in the eyes of students, parents and the public.

# October 13th

In my morning seminar, I realise this generation of students has defined feminism very differently to mine. W, a mature female student, waxes about a new kind of dating website that sounds to me like it facilitates sex work. The site invites young women and older men to agree on 'arrangements.'

These include the 'sugar daddy' offering to pay for a meal out or a shopping spree. The 'sugar babe' is not asked to specify what she will provide in return... probably because that really *would* be sex work.

At the end of her talk, I ask the student how she feels morally about this venture.

'Awesome idea. It's empowering for women.'

'Not at all degrading?'

'Naah, it's perfect for students. If we can use our sexuality to earn a bit of cash, why not? It's better than working in Tesco.'

I turn to the rest of the class. 'By show of hands how many of the women here agree with that?'

Six out of seven do.

'Don't be such a prude!' jokes a male student who has spotted my perplexed look. He then picks up his pen, turns to W and asks, 'Can you just tell me that web address again?'

That kind of talk would have got this male student a slap on the cheek when I was a student. Feminists took a dim view of bawdy, chauvinist comments.

# October 14th

I attend a 'lecture' given by a colleague to our first-years. It is the least academically rigorous outing since Trump University. The first half is a series of dreary anecdotes about their mediocre career in corporate video production, replete with photos of them shaking hands with Z-list celebrities from the 2000s. The second half purports to be an analysis of the current state of TV news. It lacks any scholarly references and is dripping with inaccuracies about ownership and regulation. By the end I feel I would have learned more by drilling a hole in my head and pouring my brains down the loo. From the looks of the students' faces, they feel the same way.

# October 15th

Another 'lecture,' this time by a guest speaker who entertains on cruise liners. It's one thing to bombard your audience with management consultant platitudes like 'we need to be both team players and individual innovators' but quite another to machine-gun them with metaphors that make no sense – and to repeatedly mispronounce the names of famous people. Apparently, techno-feudal robber barons like 'Mark *Zuckerman*' and 'Jeff *Beenos*' got to where they are today by 'thinking in 3D' and being 'conceptual cosmonauts.' The speaker doesn't define any of these terms, so the Q&A descends into Dadaist chaos with members of the enormous crowd giving their own interpretations. 'If you want to be a conceptual cosmonaut,' asks one, 'do you need to train with NASA first?'

'Err... yes, probably,' says the guest speaker. He can hardly disagree, since he has no idea what he means by that phrase either.

'I'm a designer,' says another. 'Would you say that thinking in 3D relates to the method of turning your pen and ink drawings into, say, a virtual reality app?'

'Err... yes, that too.'

This is a dark week for intellectual standards at our university

# October 19th

Always willing to cater to my students' needs – within reason – I ask at the start of my lecture whether everyone can see my slides.

'No,' shouts one girl at the back.

'No problem,' I say. 'Let me increase the magnification. How about that?'

'Still can't,' she says.

'How about this?'

'No.'

I take a deep breath. Before I can ask what else I can do for her, she says, 'I'm blind.'

Awkward laughter ripples through the theatre. I blush.

# October 20th

Labour-allocation planning meeting. If it sounds a bit Soviet Union, it is. The time we lecturers are assigned for our tasks bears no relation to reality. Two hours' prep per lecture? Ten minutes to mark each submission? Whoever's dreamed this up has never been inside a classroom. They sure as shit haven't taught in one.

Managers who devise lame policies like this do little else the rest of the time. Therefore, they are easily replaceable or worse – often nobody notices when they go off sick for months. Sometimes when they disappear, we become a more streamlined outfit. Yet they are paid way better than those of us who generate the university's revenue through teaching and research.

# October 22nd

I receive an email from our new IT system informing me about low student 'engagement'. This means that they haven't been turning up to class and/or haven't been logging on to our virtual learning environment (VLE). The first student I contact tells me she's attended every lecture and seminar so far this semester. She always swipes her ID card on the sensors beside the classroom doors – except the sensors have been broken for three weeks. The second one, who I know is conscientious, says he doesn't read the ebooks and articles on the VLE because he seeks them out for himself in the library or on Google Scholar. 'Fair enough,' I reply. The third student says they've been off sick with social anxiety disorder since last year. I imagine being lightly bollocked for not turning up has done wonders for said disorder.

Every new system introduced since I started working here – from an interactive database of student information to a travel booking application – has been useless. They cannot be navigated without two months' training – which is never provided. Everyone knows this, to the point of telling endless jokes about it. But there's never been a public discussion about why these systems came about. This despite everyone being fully aware that some higher-up signed off a lucrative contract with an outsourcing company… without apparently checking whether the system worked.

# October 24th

To a conference somewhere in the UK. If academics are already weird, then conferences make them even weirder. My colleague and I give our talk – to a grand audience of three – early in the morning. We're then free to listen to others'. I've been to enough of these gigs to know the archetypes.

There's always a mildly deranged older woman who goes into gruesome detail about the history or cultural representation of menopause, death from pregnancy or female genital mutilation. Then she will announce that, in the 'interdisciplinary' way that funders like, she has worked with a 'creative practitioner' to produce a sound collage/interpretive dance routine/rock opera/virtual reality experience that will 'transfer knowledge' about hot flushes and bleeding vaginas to non-academic audiences. Such a scholar cornered me at one after-conference party two years ago and kept squealing this refrain at me: 'The things these men did to their poor *fannies!*'

Her male counterparts are usually rakish types with a cheeky disdain for wokeness, though not expressed so publicly that Twitter users will gather with ropes and torches. Prof Laddy McBoomer (a lot of them tend to be Scottish or from the north of England) will trace a suitably masculine theme – masturbation, bareknuckle boxing, dog fighting – from early literary texts up to *Viz* magazine. This is probably due to the terms of their grant stipulating that they can't just bang on about poets who died 400 years ago because almost nobody outside of academia cares about them anymore, whereas some people outside of academia care about *Viz* magazine.

# October 25th

Conference day two. I see a lot of earnest young PhD students whose talks all follow this structure:

Part 1 – 'I read a load of nasty right-wing articles, tweets, books – or watched a load of nasty right-wing documentaries or YouTube content.'

Part 2 – 'This material is nasty to women/LGBTQ+ people/people of colour/poor people.'

Part 3 – 'We need more regulation to stop the creators of this material being so nasty. I might have got an MP interested in asking a parliamentary question about how to stop these creators being nasty.'

Part 4 – 'Thank you. Any questions?'

While the intention's worthy, the delivery and content aren't very sophisticated. I'm left pondering why the speaker didn't discuss, say, the rhetorical devices used in this material or how its nastiness might be determined by audience expectations or the values of media proprietors. In other words, where's the analysis?

These talks also avoid firm conclusions or effective solutions. In the late afternoon, I watch an earnest young academic relate an absorbing history of 20th-Century Eastern European newspapers. The problem is, the speaker has nothing to say about what any of this means socially or politically – then or now.

They might be afraid to do so. For a start, there's a general failure of political imagination. Whether you call it the 'end of history' or 'capitalist realism,' our age is running low on alternative ideas about politics, culture and society. Instead, there are only bland proposals to tweak this or that feature of the status quo. Or, just as likely, the modern academic will refuse to take a moral or political position at all – for if you do, you might not attract funding from corporations whose PR departments flinch at the first whisper of bad publicity. Moreover, most universities these days have Orwellian rules against being 'brought into disrepute.' This is code for anyone doing or saying anything that might reflect badly on the institution and blunt its competitive edge in the feverish marketplace for student fees and the remaining crumbs of state funding.

If those aren't deterrents enough, scholarly careers can and have been destroyed by social media pile-ons and rabid student campaigns. While tabloid newspapers are obsessed with 'woke' cancel culture, there's almost no coverage of academics who get hounded for criticising Churchill, the monarchy or the armed forces. We like to think that only in Iran or North Korea do academics lose their jobs for having opinions that the state despises, but in 2021 Bristol University sacked a sociology professor and Islamophobia expert, David Miller, over his criticisms of Israeli settler colonialism. An independent report from a top lawyer – a QC, no less – had determined that Miller's comments were lawful, but a disciplinary hearing 'found Professor Miller did not meet the standards of behaviour we expect from our staff' and he was sacked with immediate effect.

Piers Robinson, professor of politics, society and political journalism at Sheffield University was another academic who fell out of the ever narrower Overton Window[1] of acceptable thought. Colleagues and students lambasted him for 'promoting conspiracy theories' and for being 'dangerous.' Professor Robinson had expressed scepticism about British foreign policy, particularly towards the Syrian War, and praised a book questioning the origin of the 9/11 terror attacks as 'diligent and painstaking.' Faced by a campaign from inside his own institution that was amplified by a front page story in the *Times,* he resigned his chair in politics, society and political journalism at the University of Sheffield in 2019, citing 'professional goals and personal circumstances.'

Lower-ranking academics on casual contracts are even more vulnerable to expulsion for thought crime. TJ Coles, a prolific left-wing writer on topics from Brexit to the history of misinformation, was removed from his role on an externally funded research project at Plymouth University on nebulous charges of advocating 'outlandish conspiracy theories.'

Shorter-term suspensions are another disciplinary measure. Sheffield Hallam University cancelled one of its own media lecturer's classes in 2022 after online outrage at her defence of pro-Palestinian student activists. Shahd Absulama, a third-generation migrant from Gaza, was subjected to a high volume of racialised abuse online. She was only reinstated in her role after fellow activists, academics and trades unionists came out in solidarity with her, though eventually left anyway.

---

[1.] In political contexts: the spectrum of ideas on public policy and social issues considered acceptable or viable by the general public at a given time.

Not that the left is blameless for its own version of cancel culture. In this age of growing inequality, climate devastation and a growing nuclear threat, it seems negligent to devote one's time to hassling someone on Twitter for using the wrong word to describe someone else's ethnic group or gender identity. As the American left academic Ben Burgess puts it, we're 'cancelling comedians while the world burns.'

# October 26th

Increasingly miserable in my current role, I apply for a job at an institution in a foreign country. If I'm successful, I'll get not only a large salary increase but a discretionary research budget equivalent to £50,000 a year. In the UK, you'd have to be king of the hill at Oxbridge to access that kind of dough. The foreign institution is fully private and well resourced, judging from the sleek, spanking new architecture of its business school, law school and cosmology department. Its lecturers are housed in a salubrious apartment complex with attached gym, swimming pool, restaurants and other amenities. I'm not married, I have no kids and so have nothing tying me down to the UK – certainly not the crappy gig I have at the moment.

# October 28th

H comes to see me after a lecture. He has several disabilities and has been trying since the start of term to contact our learning support team about obtaining some software that will make his laptop more user-friendly. After dozens of unreturned calls and emails without reply, he finally received an email from the team which sent him into a tailspin of anxiety. It advised him to undergo a support needs assessment, which can only be arranged externally to the university and would cost him the best part of £300. He can't afford that – he comes from a single-parent, working-class family. When he tells me this, I wonder why on Earth we as a department can't pay for it. We probably spend more on treasury tags each month.

I email our HoD on his behalf to request the funds. I get a lame, slippery-slope argument back: `If we did that for one student, we'd have to do it for them all.`

I reply: `But how many students request this every decade, let alone every year?`

# October 29th

I email H to tell him that I'm still waiting on my HoD to respond to the request. What I don't tell him is that it's a favoured tactic of management round here to simply ignore a straight question. For them, it provides plausible deniability. They don't ever say 'no,' so can't be accused of callousness. Nor do they say 'yes,' meaning they've stuck to the rules and guarded their budget.

I end my email with an offer to pay the £300 out of my own pocket.

H replies that his local authority has agreed to stump up for it. This is good news, of course. It also shows that, comparatively, his university is a lot tighter.

# October 30th

F, a student, submits an unsettlingly articulate – or as articulate as these things can ever be – defence of far-right conspiracy theories. He's harnessed the usual paranoid fantasies about Muslims taking over the UK, universities being invaded by froth-mouthed Bolsheviks and the strings of the global banking system being tugged by a race of wandering, cosmopolitan, hook-nosed, money-grabbing reptilians... who definitely aren't Jews.'

I think it best to see him in person. I haven't done so yet. Like a lot of students, even though he is formally enrolled on my unit, he hasn't attended a single class since the start of term. His appearance is unprepossessing and he has a nervous tic that looks like he is repeatedly rolling his eyes at me... or he may well be just repeatedly rolling his eyes at me. Before we begin, I glance down his essay to refresh my memory and want to say to him, 'All this bile because you haven't lost your virginity yet.' Instead, I calmly ask him to supply evidence for his claims.

F says, variously, that he got his 'data' from Facebook, Twitter or [insert name of dubious website]. At other points he asserts that a proposition is 'common knowledge, right?'

'I don't think Nazi scientists inventing AIDS is common knowledge,' I reply.

'It's in [insert name of another dubious conservative website].'

'Does this site have any fact-checking or editorial processes whatsoever?'

He shrugs. 'Yeah. Probably. You said yourself in class that the mainstream media make mistakes all the time and that ideology can get in the way of the facts.'

'How do you know what I said when you haven't been to any of my classes this year?'

'You said it *last* year. And the year before.'

'So very sorry to be repetitive. Can you give me some examples of this media misinformation?'

'Coverage of wars, Corbyn, stuff like that.'

'This is true.'

'So in the end don't people just trust the source that they already agree with?'

'Within reason. The source must reflect reality to some extent. The media bias for Israel or against Jeremy Corbyn is not on the same scale as fabricating a story about...' I glance down at his doggerel. 'Gareth Southgate secretly being a twelve-foot, shape-shifting lizard.'

'*Woke* lizard,' he corrects me.

'Woke lizard, I beg your pardon.'

'Well... well... all kinds of things people think are mad one day end up accepted as true later. Look at Galileo – people said he was mental because he thought the Earth was round.'

F's getting het up and I need to defuse the situation. But I can't help but ask him, 'Do *you* think the Earth is round?'

'I don't know,' he says. 'Who *really* knows?'

'I think we do *really* know,' I sigh.

'People *thought* they knew Galileo was wrong.'

'You have to look at the social and historical context. Galileo used the scientific method, which went against the dominant religious worldview of his time.'

'So truth is linked to power?'

'What gets pushed as the truth does. These conservative websites your essay keeps citing are visible and widely believed because they've got money and power behind them. The right-wing think tanks behind these sites are funded by billionaires while other billionaires own most of our newspapers. *That's* how power comes into the equation.' I look back through his essay, trying to maintain a straight face. 'But that doesn't mean the Sandy Hook shooting was *actually* staged by the US government or that Hollywood is run by a cabal of satan-worshipping paedophiles.'

# October 31st

I had no idea our VC has a sense of humour until today, when he decides to let us know – on Hallowe'en, no less – that a 'consultation' and 'audit' are about to take place in advance of 'restructuring' the uni's course administration.

The upbeat tone of the first sentence, which enthuses: 'Let me express my deep personal gratitude to our colleagues in X or Y department for the important work they do,' is a characteristic portent of bad news.

# November 2nd

I attend the decidedly unglamorous unveiling of a new logo for our university. It takes place in our refectory where balloons and decorations have been tied to display cabinets of pasties and doughnuts. When the VC opens a pair of velvet curtains, we find that the logo looks like a 1970s cigarette brand. To add insult to injury, all members of staff are given a blazer badge displaying the logo.

Over white wine that tastes like hand sanitiser, I chat to colleagues who teach design. They are stunned that their input was never sought during the process of creating the logo. One, who had advance sight of it, tells me that he shared it with his students and set them the task of designing a more attractive one. They managed it in 10 minutes.

From someone in finance I learn that the cost of adding the new logo to all our corporate stationery, documentation and online platforms will approach £1.5 million.

# November 5th

H comes to see me again after class. In what is becoming a depressingly repetitive occurrence, he hasn't been able to contact our learning support team. Having completed the support-needs assessment, now he needs that piece of accessibility software.

I tell him we'll go over the road to the learning support office together. We're greeted by a near-catatonic receptionist with an ageing-rock-chick vibe. She informs us that no one is working in the office today.

'Are they working from home?' I ask.

She checks an online calendar. 'Yeaaaaaah.' As she extends the vowels, she tips her head back and closes her eyes. Is she stoned? On diazepam? 'One of them is working today,' she says. 'But only until 2.30, love.'

'That's no good, it's 2.28 now,' I say.

'Yeaaaaaah.'

'When you say "one of them," how many are there in total?'

'Two, love.'

'Only two?'

'Yeaaaaaah. And they're part-time. It's probably best to phone them another time, love.'

'Been trying to do that for weeks,' H hisses.

'Did you get through to them, love?'

'Obviously not.'

'Did you leave a message?'

'Loads of them.'

'Did they phone you back?'

'Of course not,' I intervene. 'Otherwise we wouldn't be here looking for them, would we?'

The receptionist glares at me. 'There's no need to take that tone with me; I'm just trying to help. Now how about trying to email them?'

H opens his mouth to respond, but I suggest we leave it, for the sake of our collective sanity.

We must have caused enough of a scene to prompt some bureaucratic machinery somewhere to clunk into motion, for that evening H emails me to say he's been given an appointment by the learning support team to go and collect the software. The only minor impediment is that the appointment's been booked for a bank holiday Monday. Only in a university could people in charge of learning support be so dull-witted.

# November 6th

At another public-facing event I get stuck with a dean. They are eye-wateringly ignorant. As we drink white wine – this time with a tang of petro-chemicals – they tell me that a local romance novelist is their favourite writer of all time. I tried to read one of this author's books and got ten pages in before flinging it across the room. The dean then says that, upon retiring, they want to write a memoir of all the 'madcap things' they've experienced in HE over 40 years. I agree it is a good idea and about time the campus novel popularised by David Lodge and Kingsley Amis is updated for the neoliberal era of the university. The dean looks bewildered. I assume they haven't understood at least one of the words or phrases I used. My bet is on 'campus novel' or 'neoliberal' rather than 'updated' or 'university' – but you never know.

The further up the university hierarchy you look, the thicker people get. It's like a parody of Darwinian selection – survival of the dimmest.

Such imbecility should shock no one. In addition to being a dean they hold a professorship, but they almost certainly wouldn't have obtained that had they gone through the customary and fairly rigorous promotion process. Instead, they were automatically gifted the rank (and associated pay increase) by a former, more senior dean by dint of the fact they were pals and had worked together at a previous institution. Just as dodgily, the dean I am currently talking to has a sister... who has just been made head of another department in another faculty at our institution.

One doesn't need to have a PhD in psychoanalysis to know that people tend to overcompensate for their shortcomings. This dean's intellectual achievements are in inverse proportion to the extent of their self-promotion. They are highly active on social media, cynically befriending and quote-tweeting middle-of-the-road TV intellectuals and BBC commissioning editors, and have commandeered the university's press office to try to convert a handful of mediocre publications into a golden public profile.

This dean is not alone in their wretchedness. An essential part of what Peter Fleming dubs 'the academic star-complex' is that 'fame is no longer a by-product of intellectual praxis but his or her [the academic star's] primary *raison d'être*.' The public today are 'interested in academics who seek to commodify their expertise and promote themselves through any means possible. They have literary agents telling them how wonderful they are. A personal webpage and tailored Twitter account. They appear regularly on the international speaking circuit.'

Though the dean in question would be lucky to get a literary agent or a TED talk invite, the substantive point stands. What does come across – in big, heavy bags – from my brief encounter with them is what Fleming characterises as 'individualism… underwritten by narcissistic tendencies, with an added touch of insecurity and envy.'

# November 7th

Projection becomes today's theme too, with an email from our faculty manager piously informing me: I'm very

```
very pushed for time just now. Practically
drowning in the work. I might be able to
squeeze you in for 5 mins tomorrow, no
more than that.
```

I know for a fact this is not true. Like the VC, this role is largely symbolic: signing documents they haven't read, chairing meetings on issues they haven't been briefed on and going to long, tedious lunches and receptions with other senior bods.

The less folks have to do, the more likely they are to gush about how much they have on. J, the mind-bogglingly slothful colleague, will try to cover up his lateness and absences with car trouble or trains not running. When he's bored of a Zoom or phone call he'll say, 'I've got to run and have a tutorial with a student,' even when it's mid-August and you can hear the clink of pint glasses in his background.

'I'm knackered!' is a classic refrain of the under-employed at our uni. I don't think I've ever heard it said by a colleague who's been up all night tending to a young baby or is suffering from an energy-sapping health condition.

A concomitant of the slogger-who-doth-protest-too-much is the 'presentist.' Presentists are belly-churningly sanctimonious wretches who are keen to be seen as much as possible at their desks in our soul-destroying open-plan office, even though every work task but teaching can be completed at home thanks to the wonders of tech. Presentists will make a big deal of staying late each term-time evening and coming in during the holidays. On the communal department calendar, they'll advertise themselves as being 'in the office,' when most colleagues don't bother to indicate one way or another because, whatever location we are in, most of us are hard at work. We just don't need to show off about it.

As is to be expected, when you glance over the shoulder of a presentist they'll often be toiling away... playing a game of *Clash Royale* or checking football scores. They are also invariably the ones who are most likely to enter into an hour-long chat about a topic completely unrelated to work. Generally, presentists will have impeccably tidy desks. A head of a department in another institution nearby once haughtily declared that a Spartan desk was the emphatic signifier of an employee's hard work and efficiency. I'd say the opposite: busy people tend to make a mess because they're using the objects on their desk.

# November 8th

Academics can be odd people, who do little to dispel the stereotypes the non- academic world has about them by being punch-earningly pedantic. In a traumatisingly dull meeting, I am interrupted by a professor when I use the term 'reading week.'

'I think you'll find it's now called 'reflection week,' he spits. '*Every* week should be reading week!' He then launches into a five-minute disquisition on how, when and why the university opted to change the terminology. I wish him a sticky end courtesy of rusty medieval torture devices.

# November 9th

I finish marking the first assessments for this academic year. There's been a record amount of plagiarism. Audacious, seeing as the digital platform to which the students submit work easily detects nicked material. My AO and I turn one of the tutorial cupboards into an 'incident room' where we question five suspects in turn. We feel like detectives interrogating hoodlums in a gangster movie, although uni regulations preclude us from grabbing our suspects by the scruff of the neck, sticking the barrel of a .45 in their mouths and shouting obscenities.

Even without duress, two of the students confess and break down in tears. They all give mental distress as a motive/reason/excuse. This highlights a dilemma at the withered, barely beating heart of modern HE: after centuries of lecturers not giving a toss about student wellbeing, we're now much more sensitive to it – as we ought to be – but should we forgive students *all* their trespasses because they are depressed or anxious?

In the afternoon, I receive an email containing allegations of sexual harassment made against one of my male tutees. He's said he's neurodivergent and so can't appreciate the impacts of his behaviour on others. Moreover, he claims he was sexually abused as a child. I'm glad I'm not the one who has to decide on the extent of his culpability. That said, I can't help but think the system is flawed.

# November 11th

I think again of moral responsibility when I receive unpleasant emails from another dean, one whom I shall call Dean Doom. They have been described as 'the laziest academic in the infinite story of the cosmos' by a union rep friend. Worse than that, they are probably a sociopath. The only positive contribution they ever could have made to academia was to have never entered it.

It having been made plain to me that I will soon suffocate in the academic quicksand if I don't hurry up and obtain outside funding, I've been working on a British Academy bid for the best part of a year and am on the cusp of sending it off. For much of that time Dean Doom has been absent, their duties covered by other colleagues. But they have just returned to work and are keen to reassert their authority by suddenly sticking their oar into my bid. The way in which they do that would shame a toddler.

They begin by asking me why I haven't had my bid peer-reviewed internally. I have, I reply, and they were copied into the results three months ago. They don't know that because they don't read emails or listen to a word anyone else ever says. In an increasingly pathetic attempt to retain the professional high ground, they write back. `But this bid was not independently peer reviewed.`

To which I reply, `Yes it was. The internal peer review college is, by definition, independent.` What I don't write is that it says the same in the email... which they didn't read.

Their credibility fast collapsing, they change tack. Even if it has been peer reviewed, I should have been involved in it much earlier.

I tried to involve them in it much earlier by sending them a draft. They ignored it.

I've now read the bid, they continue, and there are numerous flaws in it.

I find this hard to believe – both that they have read the bid and that there are numerous flaws in it. Could you tell me what these problems are? I write back.

I'm extremely busy right now. I'll let you and M work on that. However, I must insist on reading through the final draft before it is submitted.

M and I have already worked on it. For ages. And I have drafted it with the help of no fewer than seven other colleagues. I decide to be brave and push back at what feels like borderline bullying.

I have followed all the necessary protocols, I write. These additional requests are unreasonable and causing me a great deal of stress.

I wasn't able to make more of an input into this bid because I was terribly ill in the summer, they reply. They are now trying to make *me* feel bad about challenging her because they have been ill and my correct attitude should be one of compassion.

# November 12th

Open day for potential students who have put us as their second choice or are undecided. As I walk in to work, I'm hassled by an emaciated bloke in an army surplus jacket with shaved head and wild, zipping eyes.

'Why are you fuckin' laughin'?' he sneers.

I take out my earphones. 'I'm listening to something funny on my phone.'

'No you're not, you're laughing at me. 'Cos you're a posh cunt and you think you own this place. I bet you wasn't even born round here.'

I keep moving, he follows me.

'You wasn't even born round here!' he shouts.

The encounter says a lot about the 'town and gown' dichotomy here. One university building is smack bang in the middle of a government child-poverty hotspot and a concrete jungle housing addicts and benefit-dependent families. There's bound to be resentment towards staff and students who are better off – or appear to be so – and dress and talk and walk differently. Other than the occasional public event that lecturers like me put on, the university makes no effort to engage with the local community.

# November 13th

I attend a REF workshop. The REF is a national audit of research going on in universities that's conducted by the government every few years. This is to determine how best to allocate pitiful amounts of public money to the sector. The workshop is hosted by an external expert. We are told that our own research contributions must conform to certain criteria. *Impact* is one I can't get my head round. All the examples given by the expert seem to involve validating or supporting the status quo. You'll get props for carrying out research for House of Commons Select Committees, explicating EU policy in a newspaper or magazine, or your work being cited in the in-house journals of multinational corporations. I want to ask how often Coca-Cola cites scholars who point out how bad Coca-Cola is for you, but I know the answer already.

Moreover, the quantity of 'hits' and 'likes' is seemingly more important than the academic quality of the contribution. We are shown a video clip of a history professor speaking briefly on a BBC4 documentary about Victorian cookery. The remarks are so perfunctory that anyone could have made them after skim-reading Wikipedia. However, the academic scored highly on *impact* because the clip went viral and was seen by thousands of people who aren't academics. But what *actual* impact does that prove? Did it *really* change anything?

In my first year of teaching, I went to see a guest talk by a senior lecturer based at a Russell Group university. He was handsome, charismatic and communicated well. He was sociable enough to have a drink afterwards with all three of the people who came to watch him. Over a hastily slurped lager he announced that he was getting out of academia and into TV to 'make some proper money.' I happened to see him appear on a programme a few months later and, again, it was Ladybird-book-level stuff.

A further snag is that the REF is arguably unfit for entire subject areas. In 2013, the academic Nigel Warburton condemned the REF's narrow-minded 'measuring and quantifying' of his discipline, philosophy. 'Philosophers are struggling to find ways of describing what they do as having impact as defined by people who don't seem to appreciate what sort of things they do,' he said. He then bemoaned 'the short sightedness, the petty bureaucracy, and the often pointless activities that are creeping into higher education' before resigning from his position as an Open University professor of philosophy. Ooh, to have that luxury.

Then there's how the REF figures in the general dive in academic quality. The pressure to publish or perish has pushed researchers – and high-profile ones – to cut corners and even fake it. An investigation by the star journal *Nature* found that 70 per cent of researchers failed to replicate the findings of another scientist's experiment. Whereas in the arts and humanities such sloppiness only dents public trust and academic reputations – which is bad enough – in science it can have lethal consequences. In 2012, a *British Medical Journal* survey revealed that 13 per cent of medical researchers knew of colleagues who had indulged in 'inappropriately adjusting, excluding, altering or fabricating data.' I wouldn't want to be one of their patients. Equally worrying, scholars at the University of Virginia found that only two out of the five landmark cancer studies they analysed were replicable. I wouldn't want to neck any drugs developed from these careless investigations.

I'm about to ask what REF panellists like our guest speaker are doing about such a grim situation, when a senior colleague interrupts me. 'Sorry to cut you off but lunch has arrived.'

# November 14th

We email our verdicts to the plagiarism suspects. While they've all been 'found guilty', the fallout won't necessarily be negative. After all, one can sometimes copy whole chunks of someone else's work accidentally. In summer 2023, a humanities professor at Cambridge was found to have copied entire pages of an undergraduate's essay in an article he wrote for a top peer-reviewed journal. The professor vigorously denied that he was guilty of misconduct and a university disciplinary found that the plagiarism was 'the product of negligent acts but was not deliberate.' He was not punished. With his reputation entirely unblemished, he still teaches at the third best university in the world.

We tell our guilty students that they have failed this module. But the good news is that they'll get the chance to re-submit work in the summer and pass the year that way. Nobody is allowed to fail. Why? Perhaps because our university is dependent on student fees for 92 per cent of its income.

When I was an undergraduate, I befriended someone I'll call K. He was studying a different subject, but we bonded over a shared love of techno music. At the end of the first year, we said our goodbyes and planned to meet again in the new year. Come October I couldn't find him anywhere on campus. I soon found out that he'd failed the first year of his IT course and been kicked out. Whether K had stayed on as a student or not, the university got its funding. There was no incentive for them to put a lumphammer to academic standards. There is now.

At the same meeting, we read about a recent policy change that makes us question the very fabric of reality itself. Self-plagiarism is no longer an offence. So, in theory, this means that a student could earn a degree by submitting more or less the same paper over and over again for different modules.

# November 15th

In another research meeting, I hear the professor – who pedantically corrected me on the terminology surrounding reading week – fire off a volley of words and phrases that are surely no longer acceptable in polite discourse, especially not in a seat of learning that's supposed to follow principles of respect and dignity.

'We're in danger of being *crippled* by these new GDPR directives. It's *mental*. To have any chance of making them work, *Chinese walls* will have to be erected.' I wonder if he's doing this for a bet. Then it dawns on me that he is just an archaic boor.

# November 16th

H gets into class early and I ask him how everything's going.

'Yeah good, thanks. Can use my laptop now and I'm keeping on top of the workload.'

I notice a faint black bruise along his left cheek. Awkward as it is, I feel I have a duty of care to ask him about it.

He rotates his head away from me, as if trying to hide the wound. 'It's nothing.'

'H, come on, please tell me. I can help.'

'I was… attacked.'

'What the f—? Why?'

'I don't know. It was an older bloke, off his face. He shouted "benefit cheat" and started hitting me.'

'Where did it happen?'

'In the street, in broad daylight.'

He lifts his T-shirt and there are more bruises on his chest and abdomen.

'Please tell me someone called the police.'

'Aren't many police about these days.' He smiles mournfully. 'The guy got a good headstart but they arrested him in the end.'

'Good.'

'Not really. He might not even get a prison sentence if he has a smart enough lawyer.'

What kind of a world is it where a grown man can beat up a young adult – a child, really – because they are disabled? I don't know what else to say to him. I feel like the minor achievements we've made together – getting him his assessment and his software – have paled into insignificance.

# November 17th

I visit our VLE to view a module I used to teach on – and indeed created from scratch. All my slide shows have been posted, except my name on them has been replaced by the now-module head's.

I mention this to a friend who teaches in another discipline in our faculty. He says he's being constantly ripped off by others he's worked with on large research projects. They are all now readers and professors – while he remains a lowly lecturer. He must be missing a trick.

# November 18th

Working in HE you notice certain words or phrases get faddy over the course of a few months or even several days. This week's phrase *du jour* is 'taking individual responsibility'. It's used this morning by our department accounts manager in a snotty email to me about a claim I made for a £10 train ticket six months ago.

Then this afternoon, someone else says in a Zoom meeting, 'All of us together have to take individual responsibility for equality and diversity here in the university'. People who marched against Margaret Thatcher back in the day now talk exactly like her, and our institution is, in truth, impervious to the Conservative virtues of self-reliance and decisive action. Students rarely seek knowledge off their own bat, preferring to recycle what they are told by lecturers in the few classes they attend. When I point out SPAG (spelling, punctuation and grammar) errors in my feedback on their essays, students can't be bothered to look up what a comma splice or a passive construction is, so they ask me for 'the answers'. In fact, they often simply expect lecturers to dream up a thesis for them. The concept of individual responsibility is just as alien to many of my colleagues. The slowness, buck-passing and jobsworthery you are greeted with when making a request for, say, a box of staples would impress the staff of a co-operative tractor factory in 1930s Moscow.

# November 19th

In the morning I read through essay drafts submitted by two students who have chosen an almost identical topic to write about. They're friendly with one another in class, so I assume they've studied together and divided the research between them. It's an intriguing improvisation on the plagiarism riff – except I can't really bust them for that specific violation since they've taken enough care to ensure the two essays are different enough to just about get away with it. It's quite an achievement, really, to have spent all that time finding synonyms and alternative figures of speech. Indeed, it would have taken about the same amount of effort for them to have written essays on different topics.

It gets me thinking about how ubiquitous plagiarism is in our culture. Top academics and public intellectuals hardly lead by example. The most charitable excuse for such high-profile plundering is that these VIPs are so very important that they delegate a lot of their labour to hired researchers – and then neglect to re-write the passages provided to them. There are many cases of this and you can probably think of some. Most recently, Rachel Reeves, the Labour politician, apologised after her book on female economists featured passages of other people's work without proper referencing. She had researchers working on her book but chose not to blame them.

A distant relative of mine used to work in publishing and their job for a while was to compile popular nonfiction books of twee stories about dogs, furniture, food and other topics. My relative would trawl the media for these stories, re-write them slightly and put them in these anthologies. Okay, so this wasn't verbatim copying, but it was a form of 'borrowing.'

Anecdotes of plagiarism are all just a google away. Is it any wonder, then, that our students might think, 'If these people can get away with it, why can't I?'

# November 20th

From time to time, some of my classes go well and this afternoon's is one of them. I believe it was long ago that the lecture was determined by experts to be just about the least effectual teaching method, yet it continues to dominate HE. Few of us can pay attention to someone talking at us for more than twenty minutes, unless that someone is a brilliant stand-up comic – and 99 per cent of lecturers are not that. Instead, I've tried to heed the advice of the educationalist Geoff Petty, who rightly argues that we 'learn by doing,' and the belief of others far cleverer than me that pedagogy in the arts and humanities should be about open discussion, with no right or wrong answers and everything up for evaluation and re-evaluation.

I luck out today with a group of relatively confident students. Getting kids to speak up in class – let alone say something coherent – is hard enough, since the lion's share of them went to state schools where you're not taught public speaking. In fact, if state schools today are anything like the one I went to, you were repeatedly told to shut up and to not 'answer back.' The privately educated, on the other hand, are trained for positions in public life – because they *sound* authoritative, even when lying.

The students in my class today are not only making intelligent contributions to the debate, but are courteous towards one another and prepared to revise or nuance their opinions in light of an opposing argument. I barely get a word in edgeways but this lively discussion is surely better than me simply reading out information which they are then expected to commit to memory and regurgitate. And it certainly beats what many of my other students do in tutorials, which is ask me what they can do to get a first. To which I respond, 'You need to submit a piece of work that is cogent, engaging and based on ideas that are unique to you.'

'Ideas like what?'

'Well if I tell you that, then those ideas would be unique to *me*, not you.' But then of course I do go ahead and give them my ideas anyway, because I'm a soft touch.

I guess they've been influenced by a wider cultural trend: the hankering for the hack, the shortcut, the path of least resistance. Why read a book or grapple with a complex abstract concept when you can get a synopsis of such things on TikTok or YouTube? Having patience, investing time and focusing on an object of enquiry is hard work. It's harder work still if you're being distracted by a cornucopia of apps, screens, sounds and images that are essential to modern existence. I'm all for HE trying to adapt to this brave new world. Trouble is, we mostly haven't. It took a global pandemic that killed seven million people to drag most of us in the sector kicking and screaming into the digital world. Three months before Covid-19 struck, a colleague mentioned they were trying to develop short online learning courses that our university could offer to a potentially international student market. He was laughed out of every meeting he proposed this to – until we were all forced to stay at home and shift our teaching onto Zoom and Microsoft Teams. Now that colleague has his dream job at an American university developing virtual curricula.

In this afternoon's session, the mature students play a valuable role. Not only do they speak up, thereby encouraging their younger peers to do the same, but they are generally more conscientious and original in their thinking. Perhaps Oscar Wilde's dictum that 'youth is wasted on the young' can be converted to 'education is wasted on the young.' I was much more committed to intellectual endeavour when I did my PhD in my late twenties than when I did my first couple of degrees aged 18–22.

Mature students have lived a little longer than the others and seen more of the world. They've had a chance to be inspired by life – or moved to puzzlement or fury by it; all of which can make for compelling creative and critical work.

# November 21st

A student emails me and some of her other lecturers to inform us that she won't be attending the next three weeks of classes. That's more polite than simply not turning up to them, which is what most of her peers do. She says she will be having surgery, and that would be enough for us to know she isn't skiving. She then proceeds to explain in teeth-gritting detail the operation on her bladder that's due and her expected route to recovery. On the one hand, I wish she wrote this well for her assessments. On the other, I am put off my lunch.

Ours is an age of extreme candour. If young people aren't sharing far too much about their troubles then they're trumpeting how 'awesome' their lives are and how they're 'smashing it' and 'living their best life.' Maybe my generation started the rot. I remember idioms from the '80s such as 'floating your boat' and 'putting yourself out there.' I found it crass then, too. I'm no psychologist but when someone splatters their Facebook page with smiley face emojis, they *might just* be overcompensating for things in reality being far from jolly. I worry that the disconnect between what people advertise about themselves and what's really happening to them is fuelling the epidemic of mental distress in Gen Z.

# November 23rd

D's leaving do. She'd been a hard-working support officer in our department before being redeployed to the business and law faculty after a foolish, university-wide admin restructuring two years ago. Ever since she and others departed, our course administration has got slower, less rational and more bureaucratic. D's been so unhappy since moving to another department that she's now quit the university altogether.

People ask her – only half-jokingly – if on her last day she punched any colleagues she disliked or stole anything valuable from the office. O, a lecturer in my department, says he knows someone who left an academic job in the

UK for one in Brazil, taking his work-supplied laptop with him. His former university pursued him relentlessly for it, threatening legal action. The university ended up spending more than the laptop was worth on recouping it. The point was to exact revenge and not let the transgressor 'win.'

After enough prosecco – or, looked at another way, too much – D tells me that the courses offered in the department she's left were less rigorous than the 'Mickey Mouse' ones taught in our department. It surprises me to hear that law, business and marketing students do little writing. It's all poster presentations and multiple-answer quizzes, D claims. While our students are smeared by the media for wasting their time analysing comic books and Instagram, at least they have to construct an argument using the written word. They don't always do that in practice, but that's the aspiration.

# November 24th

I read in the newsletter that the university has shut its own bookshop. This despite everyone I know who works or studies here having signed a petition begging to keep it open. Apparently, we need the space for another IT suite.

Can a university keep calling itself such if it doesn't provide students with somewhere to buy books? In my time working here, we've also got rid of a gallery, and the philosophy and music departments. I don't know anybody who supported those decisions either.

Later, I bump into a senior colleague who tells me that, at one of the meetings I'm not important enough to attend, an even more senior colleague lost her temper and hissed, 'This is not a democracy!' At last, some honesty! On balance, I would prefer this to the cowardly two-facedness of many managers, who after making unpopular decisions try to make out that they have no choice but to act this way, or that they were compelled to do it by the 'system' or the 'higher-ups,' even though you often don't get much higher up than these very managers.

# November 25th

I bump into the same senior colleague again in the refectory at lunchtime. They tell me that all the faulty new IT systems I mentioned above have ended up costing twice their original price because the university had to hire in techies to fix them all. These were, he says, techies supplied by the same companies that supplied the original systems that didn't work.

# November 26th

N, a fellow lecturer and friend, tells me she is taking the university to an industrial tribunal. She has been bullied by a male colleague for a decade. He has exploded with rage at her on two occasions and undermined her professionally by creating a brand-new unit that covered many of the same topics as one she was already running. I guess this is down to jealousy – she is highly research active, well liked, charming and attractive. He is not any of those things.

If you exhibit talent round here, you're likely to be hated rather than appreciated. A former colleague has a theory that a lot of academics were bullied at school – we're all geeks, so this is not unlikely – and that they've borne this trauma through to adulthood. It manifests itself most toxically in self-doubt, insecurity and ruthless one-upmanship.

# November 27th

N asks if I will write a witness statement for her tribunal. I agree. She tells me she's joined an informal network of other employees – almost all women – who are currently seeking redress from the university for various abuses. An Asian female colleague in another faculty is about to arrive at a generous settlement after two years of sexist and racist harassment. One of the microaggressions against her was far from original.

'Where are you from?' asked a white colleague.

'South London.'

'But where are you *really* from?'

Another colleague, the only female in an entire department of nerdy, homosocial men, is about to get a payout for being systematically patronised, shouted at and overlooked for promotion. According to the union reps N has spoken to, such cases are frighteningly common. The national picture is similar, with investigations by the Universities and College Union having found that sexual harassment in HE is 'rife,' with women, the disabled, LGBTQ+ people and those on zero-hours contracts more likely to be on its receiving end.

The university deals with both the victims and the perpetrators poorly. One white male reader, who had 72 allegations of sexual harassment to his name from both staff and students, was allowed to leave quietly and waltz into another job at another institution. Though not on the same scale of awfulness, another white male colleague skyrocketed from lecturer to professor in the space of three years, his progress in no way hampered by the fact that he'd 'delivered' his course results in a 'comedy' Chinese accent.

As for the victims, I learn, compensation is all well and good, but it comes at the price of the recipients having to sign a non-disclosure agreement. If no one is ever allowed to talk about these wrongdoings, how can we prevent them in future?

After our meeting, I laugh darkly to myself at a sign in the foyer promoting a 'Diversity Festival.' The only diversity I can think of round here is an expansive range of bigotry, from the ignorantly offhand to the chillingly premeditated. Over the years, I've heard comments about trans students lacking sartorial style and not being convincing enough females. I've lost count of the anecdotes I've heard about women receiving unwanted flirts and propositions, and all manner of creepy comments from, once again, white cisgender men.

## November 29th

I'm reminded of the restructuring that D fell foul of when I try to solicit the help of our admin team. Nowadays, these staff members are uncooperative and officious. This may be a deliberate tactic to put lecturers off from asking for assistance – and therefore making them do some work.

I call our admin manager up about a room I taught in yesterday that isn't big enough to accommodate the full complement of the class. 'Can we book a bigger one?' I ask.

She has a strange kind of lisp which makes her pronounce 'sh' sounds as 'ss.' 'You *ssould* have requested a bigger one to the timetabling team last summer,' she says.

'I did. They still gave me a room that's too small. Look, I can see on the booking system plenty of alternatives for that same time and day slot. It'd be easy to—'

'—We *ssouldn't* really go against the timetabling team now.'

'What am I supposed to do if there aren't enough chairs for all the students?'

'Is it likely you'll get 100 per cent attendance any time soon? This isn't the most *bookiss* generation of youngsters, is it?'

'No, but that's not really the point.'

I give up and go into the stationery cupboard in our office to look for some red pens and a pair of scissors that I need for a seminar exercise. It doesn't have these items in it, nor any others of any use. It has some ancient folders that are crumbling to dust. One has 'ARW?' stamped on to its back cover. Later on, I ask the oldest colleague in my department what this means. They say it refers to 'air raid warning.' So we have items from World War II still knocking about. Bottles of Tippex are dried shut. Even if they worked, I can't think of any application they would have in a modern, largely paperless office. There's a box of rusty paperclips all bent out of shape, like they've all been fiddled with by someone with a severe nervous condition. There's also a small library of outdated student handbooks and promotional brochures for the university, some of which date back to the early 2000s.

I take a deep breath and head over to the admin office. Inside it is a much larger stationery cupboard that's full of better quality gear. The door is locked, so I go over to the admin manager to ask for the key.

She addresses me slowly and in an annoying high-pitched voice like the one particularly patronising adults use on babies. 'Not just *anyone* can go into that cupboard, you know.'

'With respect, I'm not just anyone. I'm a lecturer and I need this equipment for my teaching.' I figure that if she's going to be a condescending *ssithead*, then I can be too. 'Teaching is quite important to what we do here.'

'Don't be *waspiss* with me,' she spits. 'It *ssould* be a keyholder that lets you in. Those are the rules and I don't make them up – take them or leave them.'

Wow, I didn't know real people in real life said stuff like this. I feel like I'm in a '60s kitchen sink drama.

'If you're the keyholder can you let me into the cupboard?'

'I'm not the keyholder.'

'Who is the keyholder?'

Now I feel like we're in a particularly tedious sword and sorcery film, where the keyholder and all her orcish minions have to be defeated in order to enter the magical realm of the stationery cupboard.

'The keyholder is away today. She had to *dass* off early to collect her child from school.'

'Could we locate the key in their absence?' I look past her desk and see a bunch of keys hanging from a nail banged crookedly into the wall. 'Is that the key there, by any chance?'

'It *ssouldn't* matter whether it is or it isn't there—'

'Well, it does to me.'

I turn around and leave. What I've learned since then is that it is often easier for lecturers to source equipment ourselves – out of our own pocket.

In the late afternoon, I can't get the Dalek-sized printer working. According to colleagues, it hasn't been working for three months. Suffice to say, no one in the admin office has the first clue how to fix it. I'm given the number of the faculty maintenance department... which no one answers.

I go home that night and print what I need at my own expense.

# November 30th

A preternaturally handsome older male colleague tells me warily about a female student who is sending him nude pictures and propositioning him via Facebook. 'What should I do?' he asks.

'You should get fat and bald like the rest of us,' I say.

'If I was female and the student was male, you wouldn't be taking the piss,' he says.

I straighten my mouth.

# December 2nd

I head to the local supermarket to buy a sandwich for lunch and find that it has closed down. I walk a bit further to an independent, family-run café and find that, too, has shut. I stagger back dazed by a sense of entropy, of the university's deterioration somehow radiating out to the surrounding landscape.

That afternoon, I go to the high street near campus to buy a suit for a friend's wedding. All four of the clothes shops that were doing a brisk trade four months ago have gone bust. Fittingly, 'Ghost Town' by the Specials is playing from about the only shop left open, Poundland.

On my way out of the spectral street, I suddenly need a wee. Badly. What used to be a public toilet is no more and there are no pubs or restaurants around anymore. I pop into the office of a small bus station, which is about the only solvent business left round here.

A floorboard-skinny old geezer with white mutton-chop sideburns looks up from his phone.

'Can I use your toilet please?'

''Fraid it's closed for cleaning.'

'Do you have a staff one?'

'We do.'

I gnash my teeth. 'Can I use it?'

'No.'

'Why not?'

'Insurance reasons.'

'What do you think I'm going to do in there, paint a Banksy-style mural? Spontaneously combust when I come into contact with the hand dryer?'

'Been known to happen. Well, rude graffiti.'

'Come on, mate, have a heart.'

'Not legally obliged to provide a toilet for the public. Move along or I'll call security.'

While it'll take a while before I can relieve myself, I feel oddly relieved in another sense – I've ascertained that there are bureaucrats in the outside world whose blood runs even colder than that of their kith inside a university.

# December 5th

The scary runup to submission deadlines. This is when students you haven't seen all semester suddenly email you, panicking about not having seen you all semester and how they don't know what to do... I have a Zoom tutorial with a mature student called Y. I have long suspected she is paranoid. She's written candidly about her painful experiences of substance abuse. Although it's hard to penetrate her stream-of-consciousness style, it appears that she has spent time as a sex worker to support her habit, and has been physically and sexually abused.

I ask her if she's getting the care she needs.

'Naah,' she snorts darkly. 'They went and closed the refuge down, didn't they? And there used to be that rehab place on R-Road – that's gone too. Plus it's hard to concentrate on studying when you can't afford to eat much.'

Once again, I feel like I am mopping up the mess that is early 2020s Britain – except I'm not a social worker, doctor, psychologist or politician. 'Have you tried contacting the uni wellbeing service?' I ask.

'And wait half a year for some twat to tell me I should meditate and learn how to breathe proper? Naah.'

'Alright then, shall we look at your work?' I explain to Y that, while the material is poignant and timely, improvements need to be made to its style, structure and coherence. I explain to her as tactfully as I can that it's hard for a reader to follow one key passage because there is little punctuation.

'You wouldn't understand the point I'm making there 'cos you're a man.'

'I'm not criticising the point you're making – it's perfectly valid. It's just the way you make it that needs more work.'

'You should be much more sensitive about what you're saying to me. What I've been through is terrible.'

'I'm not disagreeing with you.'

'And I have *the right* to relate what's happened to me in the way I want to relate it. I'm not going to be dictated to by you or any other man in my life. You can see the damage that's caused, can't you?'

'I'm not trying to dictate to you, I'm trying to help you.'

'Believe you me, I've had plenty of men say they *want to* help me.'

'It's my job to help you.'

'I've heard that one too.'

I pause, feeling like anything more I say will just irritate her further.

'Well, I'm not making any changes,' Y continues. 'A lot of what you've read has already been published on a blog. I have readers whose second or third language is English, and they get it. Maybe *you're* the one who's not getting it. And you're English.'

'It's possible,' I sigh. 'But at the end of the day, I'm your lecturer and I have to grade you according to my knowledge of the formal conventions of writing. If you choose not to follow my advice then I can't promise you that you're going to get the mark you're hoping for.'

I wait for her to respond, but she just scowls off-camera.

'Let's draw this to a close and meet again next week.'

'You mean when I've calmed down?'

'No, I didn't mean or say that. It's just that, with respect, I don't think we're getting anywhere. I just seem to be upsetting you and that is not my intention.'

'Agreed,' Y snaps and turns off her Zoom.

As a lump forms in my throat, I find myself – almost automatically – scouring job vacancy websites. Gravedigging suddenly looks enticing.

# December 7th

I'm invited to give a talk about research outputs to some foreign graduate students. At the lunch afterwards I chat with a trio of African PhD candidates whose recent experiences would indicate they slipped through a timewarp to the 1950s. In fact, they attended a country fête only last week in a nearby village. After they'd enjoyed the Morris dancing and Women's Institute bake sale, a local councillor came up to them and exclaimed, 'May I just say how wonderful and bright you look. You really stand out here.'

'Yes, it looks like we're the only Black people for miles,' said one of the students.

The councillor turned scarlet. 'No, I didn't mean that. I was talking about your lovely bright clothing.' The student in question was wearing traditional Yoruba dress.

On the walk back to the train station, some inebriated villager sidled up to one of the female students and waved a Ginster's pasty at her. 'I fuckin' love Caribbean food,' he sputtered.

'I'm from Ghana,' the female student said.

He looked blank.

'That's nowhere near the Caribbean,' she explained. She looked more closely at the drunkard's pasty and noticed the packaging read 'Cajun style.' 'Cajun people are quite far away from the Caribbean too,' she added. 'But not as far away as Ghana.'

He stayed looking blank.

'We found the *real England* that day,' one of the students jokes to me.

# December 9th

Unable to sleep, I see an email come in at 3.42am from that foreign university to which I applied back in October. I have been shortlisted for the role. The interview process will be long and drawn out. It'll involve numerous meetings with various officials. I'll also be required to deliver a formal presentation so, I guess, they can work out whether I'll be a half-decent teacher. Looks like they're going to make me earn my salary boost and gargantuan research budget.

# December 10th

Student feedback committee in the afternoon. I'm here to record the concerns raised by student representatives of several courses and pass them on to the relevant colleagues. There is a shedload of complaints this semester. I'm relieved that none of them are about me or anything I'm responsible for.

First up, I'm told that students can barely understand a word S says. Unfortunately for him, he stammers, does not finish sentences and peppers his speech with 'ums' and 'ers.' Assuming English was not his first language, one Bulgarian student plucked up the courage to ask him where he came from. 'Luton,' he said.

While I note down these gripes, I don't know what I'm supposed to do about them. What *can* I say to S? I imagine he needs speech therapy or something like that, and that's not going to fix this problem in the short term, before these poor students have to try and pass his unit.

Another course representative says that B, an adjunct lecturer, insensitively responded to an email from a student saying that they wouldn't be able to attend an exam because it clashed with a close relative's funeral. There was no message of condolence from B, just a cold Ensure you get in touch with admin to arrange retaking the exam in the summer.

*It can't get worse than this*, I say to myself as the next course representative flips open their laptop. A half dozen students have complained about the 'boring as shit' lectures of U, who appears not to have updated her notes since 1992. Her 'contemporary' analyses of music videos end with those of Seattle grunge bands, while her 'brief history of videogames' culminates in *Sonic the Hedgehog 2*. Her politics must have got stuck in the past too, given that she said out loud the P-word in one lecture. And, yes, Asian students were present. In mitigation, she did not use the term in anger, she was quoting a tabloid newspaper article... from 1992. Worse than that – and the course representative seems to relish telling me this – embittered students have started a private Facebook group called 'The We Hate Dr U Club' where they share their angst about her teaching and generally take the piss out of her. I say to the representative that this is unfair on U and can they ask whoever set up the group to take it down. Let's try and deescalate this situation, please. I promise to have a word with U about her shortcomings. It's reasonable to ask a colleague to stop using racist epithets in class, but how do I communicate to them that their entire research portfolio is outdated, without embittering them?

# December 11th

I call U in the morning and she says she will apologise to the students about the P-word in next week's lecture. She points out that it's weird that these same students are happy to watch Quentin Tarantino films that are littered with N-words without complaining to Netflix or indeed ogle porn that humiliates women without grouching to Pornhub.

I don't believe I've ever given trigger warnings at the start of my own classes. It's hard to anticipate what might upset any given student at any given time. There are other contradictions, too. Reacting to a hypersensitive climate and the risk of knee-jerk reactions on social media, lecturers in other institutions have taken certain books and films off the syllabus because they represent slavery, sexual assault and suicide. But a representation of something terrible is not a moral validation of it – quite the contrary in the cases of *Twelve Years a Slave, The Color Purple* and *A Fine Balance*. We're back to that dilemma of needing to protect the welfare of students but also requiring them to recognise that the world is nasty, unfair and violent – and that a good deal of great art reflects that.

That said, I've been in that sticky situation where the visceral depiction of a traumatic or transgressive event has so offended students that it precludes the holding even of conversation. In one lecture a few years ago, I mentioned that the French philosopher Louis Althusser had murdered his wife. Even though I didn't return to this point and the lecture was entirely on his ideas about ideology, I could see from their buffeted expressions that several students had been put off anything to do with Althusser – the man or the thinker. This brings us to another problem: should the abhorrent personal lives or attitudes of a writer, artist or intellectual disqualify them from being studied? I would say not. I'd go further and urge that, if one wants to watch a movie or read a book that provides original insights into, say, the nature of evil, it might actually help if the creator of that text was a bit of a fuckhead. However, this is a controversial view nowadays, especially among younger people.

U and I riff on such stuff for ten minutes before I decide to pop the question, 'Were we like that as students?' U thinks not. In our day, if a book or film or art work was risqué and iconoclastic and kicked against received opinion, we lapped it up.

I recall being thrilled as an undergrad to discover in my university library an old history book with a fold-out board game inside it called *World Dictators' League*. It was inspired by the card game *Top Trumps* and players earned points by comparing their chosen dictators (Idi Amin, 'Papa Doc' Duvalier, Joseph Mobutu or whoever) according to gruesome criteria ('extrajudicial killings,' 'corruption,' 'suppression of free speech' and so on). Finding the publication date of the textbook to have been 1973, my mates and I concluded that the authors must have been hippie educationalists who'd intended *World Dictators' League* to be a wacky and experimental teaching method.

'If that came out now, imagine the scandal,' says U.

# December 12th

I go late into the night marking the latest batch of submissions. I come across an eerily well-written paper by someone who has never submitted a well-written paper before – or anything approaching one. I doubt this student would know the meaning of the critical terms appearing in their own submission. But is it their own? I'm aware of companies nowadays that will write you an essay on spec and for a fee. Plagiarism has gone untraceable. And now, spotting it is even tougher thanks to apps like ChatGPT that will generate a serviceable essay from a few typed commands. Who needs actual intelligence when you have artificial intelligence?

# December 13th

The day the students are supposed to give assessed presentations. Supposed to. First up is L, a slight girl with hair dyed the colour of Parma Violets, which she likes to eat in class. Rather than profess on her chosen subject, she dashes out into the corridor. I give it a few seconds and follow her. I find her weeping, fist in mouth. I'm about to reassure her when another student, R, joins us. I'm surprised that this handsome, strapping and normally confident rugby player type is struggling. I guess it takes all sorts. He is shaking and stammering. 'Oh m - m - mate, I - I - I - I - c - c - can't d - d - do it.'

I peek back through the door of the classroom to ascertain whether anyone else will be requiring emergency assistance today. It transpires that a total of five students out of 16 are too anxious to present. Because I am not a bastard – but may be a pushover – I agree that these five can, at a later date, either record their talk or deliver it to me one-to-one.

At the end of the session, I consider throttling myself with a computer lead. As a teacher, it's hard not to blame yourself for a shit-show of this magnitude. Am *I* causing all this anxiety amongst the students? Do I come over as uncaring or remote? Am I working them too hard? (No.) Do I make them nervous? Do I scare them? I'm not scary, am I? I'm a teddy bear. I think.

When I've calmed down, I mull over abandoning the assessed presentation next year. But won't that deprive the students of the life skill of communicating with others? If learned and practised, this can overcome... exactly the sort of fear that put a third of this morning's class out of action.

# December 14th

I host a pre-Christmas showcase of students' work. Memories of Prof X are triggered when a brilliant British-Palestinian student I'll call C gets up and starts denouncing other lecturers who have accepted blood money from the military-industrial complex. He is rightly miffed about his relatives in Gaza who are frequently assaulted by Israel's F-35 Lockheed Martin fighter planes – built with parts from BAE Systems.

'Thanks, C,' I sigh after he's left the stage. 'I hope your info checks out or I'll see you in debtors' prison.' But I'm only half-joking. I'm very impressed that C is one of the few students today who are active on peace and social justice causes. I wish there were more.

# December 16th

I rise at 3am for my first interview with the foreign university that's shortlisted me. Within the first few minutes, the two biggest Zoom clichés have come to pass: (1) my cat jumps onto my lap and miaows at the camera and (2) one of my interlocutors holds forth for 30 seconds before realising that he hasn't turned his microphone on.

When we get underway, my hosts afflict me with the kind of boosterism that I'd hoped was just a Western disease. A hunched, rounded man tells me how bloody marvellous his institution is, how it's this rank in that league table and all that. I find such showing off as irritating as Gyles Brandreth is.

In a jarring U-turn from the bigging-up, a young woman with braces interjects that their students do not speak English very well at all and would that be a problem for me? I want to say, 'I'm well used to that amongst my native English students.' But this doesn't seem the time or place for wisecracks.

'You would have to simplify your teaching material significantly,' says Ms Braces.

'I've taught English for speakers of other languages,' I reply.

As one, the panel nod and make a note. Meanwhile I fret about how much extra stress this might entail and how bored I might become marking *Janet and John*-level papers. On the other hand, in my limited experience of teaching abroad, I've found that students are friendlier and more committed and conscientious than British ones, for a range of reasons.

Professor Big raises the topic of research. He seems to have properly investigated me on that score and even read some of my publications. He also comments intelligently on the research project I proposed in my application form.

The panel thank me and tell me I'll need to have a further few meetings – also in the middle of the night UK time – before they can recommend me for the next stage of the application process.

# December 17th

With characteristic sensitivity and good timing, the VC announces the results of the consultation and audit. Fourteen people are going to be fired just before Christmas. At the end of his email the VC says that the uni will be offering counselling to the dumped to help them 'build resilience at this difficult time.' That should stave off eviction and pay for the kids' Christmas presents.

# Semester 2

# January 15th

I've spent the Christmas holidays soul-searching. I don't think I can stand it here anymore. Will that role at the foreign university come off? Should I quit HE altogether? If so, what else am I going to do? I don't have the training or qualifications for a 'proper job.'

I'm prompted to make a new year's resolution to start resisting the mendacity and injustice of this place by a few nasty things that happen over the next few days.

This evening, I have drinks with colleagues in the pub and the conversation turns to ancestry. When young L mentions she is Jewish, O blurts out, 'Oh, that figures.' Visibly hurt, L changes the subject to the weather.

Later on, when I'm waiting for a taxi with L, she says, 'Why would O say that? Because I have a big nose? Because he thinks I'm clever or talkative? Not penny-pinching I hope – I bought the fucker a drink.'

# January 17th

L forwards me an email trail showing Z, another colleague, accusing L of ranting and speechifying. Earlier on in the trail, L has mentioned her Jewish heritage with reference to an equality and diversity consultation.

I call L to express my sympathy. She says that Z is probably unaware of the dusty old anti-Semitic stereotypes of 'the big-mouthed Jew' or of putting 10 Jews in a room and eliciting eleven opinions – the sort of thing that Jews can say about themselves in jest, but that gentiles really can't... unless they are racist wankers.

# January 18th

The first step to realising my new year's resolution is to vote – with the majority of my fellow union members – to take industrial action. Already the right-wing press is libelling 'lazy, greedy, lefty lecturers' because we want a pay rise, though not even as high as the inflation rate, now high as Johnny Depp atop a heap of hard drugs. Teachers, nurses, junior doctors and firemen will all be joining us. This feels like an important moment, maybe on a par with the Miners' Strike. If working people don't do something about it our society will turn into a blisteringly unequal nightmare of low wages, food insecurity, meagre healthcare and state oppression.

On the same day, I attend my first meeting of our departmental EIHR (Equality, Inclusivity and Human Rights) committee. I know that breaking off our relations with the arms industry is a hard sell, so I try and explain it in basic moral terms. I start by saying that most legal and judicial systems around the world recognise that there are different grades of crime. Generally, more resources are devoted to stopping and punishing baby murderers than dog-owners who don't clear their critters' shit up – and rightly so. Likewise, if a fire engine arrives where there's a Grenfell-style tower block ablaze on one side of the street and a cigarette smouldering in a dustbin on the other, most folks of sound mind would hope they'd tackle the towering inferno first. We ought to apply the same principles, I say, to our conduct as a large organisation that has committed itself through various charters and concordats to opposing racism, sexism and other forms of human oppression. If we did that thoroughly then we would – before addressing the no-doubt-important problem of too many pale faces and penises amongst our staff and students – divest from our gun-making and gun-toting partners in order to save the lives of many people of colour – often also female, often also LGBTQ+ – from Jenin to Jersey City, Mogadishu to Manila.

The reaction I get depends on where a colleague is in the pecking order. At my level there's a degree of surprise. 'What's the extent of our relationships with these operations?' asks one with a look of genuine concern. I show them the result of a FOI I made to the university. It shows that four arms companies have invested close to £2.5 million in our research and innovation activities. Think of a recent conflict – Iraq, Afghanistan, Syria, Israel-Palestine, Libya, Yemen – and these firms will have profited from it. I mention that our university also provides training to the militaries of human-rights-smashing states in the Middle East. Saudi Arabia's war on Yemen has slaughtered 130,000 (25 per cent of whom are children) and crushed the dark-skinned, racially oppressed Muhammasheen caste.

'But we've got to live in the *real* world,' says someone higher up the pecking order.

I pause to consider what can be more 'real' than a poverty-emaciated foreign baby getting decapitated by a bullet, the profits of which are currently washing through our university's accounts.

What follows is a flurry of fallacies that seem to confirm Newcastle University lecturer Sinéad Murphy's contention that the near-abolition of subjects like philosophy from British HE has greatly dented people's ability to think.

Another gormless rectangle of a senior manager drones to me, 'Where would these ethical reforms of yours end? If we broke off ties with *all* dodgy partners who cause harm we wouldn't sell Coca-Cola in the refectory or use Monsanto-made weedkiller in the park. Before we knew it the university would collapse.' I think they call this the 'slippery slope' argument, which often enough results in conservative inertia i.e., we can't possibly do everything, so why even try to do *something*? What's worse is that I suspect this challenger is saying all this in bad faith. As an engineer, I doubt he wants to divest from oil-business funding, he's just building the slippery-slope ramp to try to shut me up.

Next up is a young woman with her hair dyed luminous green and a big badge on her lapel reading TRANS RIGHTS ARE HUMAN RIGHTS. For self-professed and self-projecting 'left-wingers' like her, the struggle for LGBT+ people, women, BAME members etc begins and ends with their having attained legal equality and a vague feeling that these people are human, after all. It does not extend to proposals like mine, which would actually prevent the deaths of such marginalised people. I am therefore the diametric opposite of astonished when she reaches for that most degraded of tautological arguments: the virtue of continuing these relationships lies purely in the fact we have *always had* such relationships. 'This institution has worked with the military for decades, so why stop that now?' It clearly hasn't crossed her mind that the same logic was – and still is – used by bigots who insisted that, since most societies throughout history have believed homosexuality is wrong, why break with tradition and make it socially acceptable? She's also probably unaware that her ideological forebears resisted the banning of colour bars and child sacrifice on the same basis.

Although by my calculation we have 15 minutes left, the chair of the meeting announces that we're out of time. In a variation of the common-sense-that-isn't-common-sense theme, the chair deploys another tautology: 'We are where we are.' It's an ugly, meaningless phrase that is wheeled out for reactionary ends. Ultimately, it's a way of re-asserting the status quo: if we are where we are, then we can't be anywhere else.

Like many bad ideas, I imagine it originated in the United States. The spoken register of HE functionaries is a bizarre blend of sporting, military and – shock horror – academic-sounding idioms. I say 'academic-sounding' because, further to Murphy's point about the intelligence bypass that has afflicted universities lately, such terms are bandied about with little care for their meaning. 'Liminality,' for example, has a specific application to anthropology and cultural studies, yet I've heard it used to refer to the ongoing maintenance of fridge-freezers in our halls of residence. Everything from plastic waste around campus to the Teaching Excellence Framework has been imbued with a 'narrative,' yet not one that would be instantly recognisable to Truffaut or Tolstoy.

The sporting metaphors have been known to burst the blood vessels of anyone who gives a fig about language. When it comes to [insert university activity/policy/priority here], we must all *step up to the plate* and *knock it out of the park* – or, in other nebulous ways, *smash it*. Individual *performance* is as important as *teamwork*. Our IT systems are *agile* and involve *sprints*. And you must show resilience if you get *athlete's foot, a verruca, a cricket ball in the testicles* or *a broken nose from a criminally insane central defender called Kev or Trev*. Alright, I made those last couple up. But they're no sillier than the real-life phrases.

As for the militaryspeak, a younger faculty member rounds off our meeting on divestment with a plea to 'send in the marines.' I don't know whether he means this literally or figuratively, since we have just been talking about soldiers and bombs killing people.

# January 19th

At lunchtime I receive an email from a colleague with a specialism in human rights law who attended the meeting yesterday. They inform me that, while they broadly agree with my gripes, a university can't be held responsible for the crimes of its partner organisations that exist geographically, administratively and jurisdictionally outside of its ambit.

I'm not so sure about that, I reply. HE panjandrums like to construct a border – that's both physical and moral – between what counts as 'there' (the Middle Eastern autocracies, wars and arms sales taking place abroad etc that the university is financially connected to) over which they say they have no control and the more positive 'here' referring to the university campus. 'Here' contains 'safe spaces' for BAME and LGBTQ+ students, and cosy, supportive 'hubs,' 'communities' and 'networks' where staff and students can expect succour and encouragement. However, this idea of spatiality is limited.

While a university may be physically bounded, in other senses its space extends to include places and events all over the world, given its 'networks of social relations,' as geographer Doreen Massey puts it. It follows that universities can't excuse themselves from the hideous things that happen in this extended 'here.' This was recognised by journalists in 2018 who intimated that the University of Birmingham was responsible for the welfare of LGBTQ+ staff and students on its satellite campus in Dubai, given the UAE's homophobic and transphobic laws.

We might also say that the line between 'here' and 'there' blurs when it comes to military technologies developed inside a British university engineering department that are then deployed in Yemen or Somalia, or an oil company that ploughs profits made from beggaring and despoiling sub-Saharan Africa into a climate denial thinktank of eccentric British academics.

I don't receive another email from that colleague.

# January 21st

L calls me to inform me that she has now been the victim of a hat-trick of microaggressions. She's been exposed to the number one, the nonpareil, the *molto meglio*, the best-of-the- best, the Rolls Royce of Jew-baiting canards: that Jews secretly control the world. This wasn't delivered to her face, though, it was told to L by G that this is the view of R, with whom L feels she gets along.

# January 22nd

In the refectory I natter with younger colleagues. They say they won't be joining the industrial action, as they 'can't afford it.' I don't know their specific financial situations, but I do know that if they did strike they'd lose about £300 from their annual salary of £51,000. I also know that they both educate their children privately, which doesn't stoke my sympathy.

But the worst of it is their hypocrisy – hypocrisy defines approaches to equality and diversity in HE. Self-declared feminists and anti-racists, these colleagues write about oppressed brown female and LGBTQ+ bodies in the Global South... yet can't get on board with our union's other key demand of the UCEA (Universities and Colleges Employers Association): an end to the colossal pay gap between male and female, and white and BAME employees in HE.

# January 23rd

I attend a huge online, all-staff meeting to discuss the scourge of Chat GPT. A cranky ex-hippie colleague warns: 'This could mean the end of higher education as we know it. With AI teaching drones probably not far away either, what place will there be for human lecturers at all?' They are actually quite sanguine about this eventuality, possibly because they're due to retire on a fat pension in a few months.

I make a brief point. Chat GPT isn't the problem. It's a tool that can be used for good or bad, like a knife can be used to sculpt something beautiful or to stab someone in the heart. Rather, we need to be asking why would students be motivated to use this software to concoct an essay for them in the first place? Surely, they should enjoy the process of doing it themselves, in the same way people enjoy cooking dinner from scratch as opposed to just putting a ready meal in the microwave. The point should be about the work *you* have put into it, how *you* have made the work *your* own. Or *should be*, if the whole experience of education hadn't been turned into an instrumentarian box-ticking exercise aimed entirely at getting a piece of paper that nominally qualifies you for a job. If the objective is simply about what happens *after* your degree finishes, then aren't you going to be tempted to take shortcuts through the degree, because the degree itself is not a priority, it's just a stepping stone to something more important. Isn't it ultimately HE's fault for pushing this ethos onto students? In other words, our fault?

As you can imagine, this final comment provokes much scowling and rolling of eyes. Once again, the promise of an open, free and wide-ranging debate quickly crumbles once the status quo – the fundamentals of how universities are run – comes into question.

## January 25th

I read in the press that our proposed new campus in Asia will never be more than a proposition, as market research has found that nobody wants to study there. The market research, along with other 'development costs,' comes to a mind-blowing £112,000. That's the equivalent of four lecturers' annual salaries flushed down the proverbial toilet. Or, to look at it another way, a fraction of that figure could fix all the toilets on campus, one third of which are out of action at all times.

What my union have dubbed 'vice chancellor's vanity projects' are even dearer at other universities. British institutions seeking to set up satellites in Malaysia and New York have lost tens of millions due, again, to not attracting enough students. One university built a satellite department in Dubai for £100 million on the proviso that its LGBTQ+ staff should keep shtum about being LGBTQ+ – or risk five years in jail.

And there's more waste coming, as UK universities prepare to spend four and a half billion pounds on shiny new gear that 'does not benefit students or staff,' as one university union sees it.

# January 27th

Up at 4am to Zoom with two senior figures in the department of the foreign university. I'm unsure of the point of this meeting as it's a retread of the interview I did back in December. I ask for some more detail on the research budget attached to the post and about the balance of research and teaching duties they are expecting. I'm told I'll have to meet with the admin manager next week to find out.

Later that morning, my AO calls me and three other lecturers attached to a first year unit into an 'urgent' meeting.

A student of colour has made a formal complaint about racism. We are mystified and mortified. When read out, the allegations are vague. The student claims that we were unavailable for personal tutorials, that we didn't update the VLE with useful information and that we failed him because he is Black. All of this is palpably untrue. We failed him because he submitted papers that were poorly written.

One of my co-accused breaks down and cries. As well she might – her partner is British-Asian and her children are mixed race. My Jewish colleague L isn't exactly elated about being called a racist, either. While I'm not a member of an oppressed ethnic minority, I'm galled by the allegations given the work I'm now doing to make the university a more tolerant place. For a moment, I consider jacking that in.

'Anyone worried about a double standard here?' I venture as we're winding the meeting up. 'If any of us were to make such a hurtful and false accusation against a student we'd be hauled up in front of a disciplinary committee. By the same token, there's a code of conduct that all our students sign up to which includes not treating their lecturers like shit.'

My AO sighs. 'I agree with you, but enforcing that is a pain.'

I know why – this student is paying our wages. And if he dislikes being bollocked for this outrageous behaviour then he might decide to drop out – and *stop* paying our wages. For that reason, my AO's email to him will be apologetic and conciliatory.

# February 1st

EIHR Committee meeting. Today's great strike against the world-historical scourges of racism, imperialism, transphobia, homophobia and sexism consists of... talking about the photos on our new marketing brochures. Most committee members believe that the more diverse the faces you put in such material, the pleasanter people will be to each other. My understanding is that images of a 'post-racial' Shangri-La only conceal – and may even perpetuate – a reality that is anything but. If nothing else, first-year students will be mightily miffed when they get here and discover that we are *not* a rainbow nation of neurodiverse Nepalese lesbians linking hands and dancing with Bedouin transmen and Orthodox Jewish dwarves.

# February 5th

I have lunch with V, a fellow lecturer. She agrees that improvements are needed hereabouts, but is pessimistic. She tells me of a HoD in another university – where her partner works – who was subjected to a vote of no confidence. Eighty per cent of the lecturers in that department were in favour of ousting him. The HoD, in turn, claimed this was bullying and complained to his superiors. Each plotter was then interviewed by a special investigator to determine their motives. Were they being vindictive or were they right to argue that the HoD was incompetent?

The bosses forced a compromise. The HoD was made to stand down and given a 'floating' management role. This translated into '£66,300 a year for doing nothing.' With salutary candour, the HoD worded it exactly this way down the pub some weeks later. And then laughed hysterically about it.

The new HoD turned out to be even worse than the one the plotters had worked so hard to depose. This is what has convinced V that universities are unlikely to reform themselves.

V adds that lobbying for change in the arts and humanities could be futile given that such departments may soon be extinct – at least outside Oxbridge and the Russell Group. She attended a HE policy conference last week where a sharp-suited spiv working in recruitment at a higher-flying 'new' university, convinced V that her subject would be abolished in the next four years. V was fazed by the exactitude of the period – *four* years rather than a *few* or *several*. She will only be in her late forties then and in no financial position to retire.

I do some research in the evening and find that there's a de facto shit-list of disciplines that have vanished from HE syllabi. Fine art, drama, music, philosophy – in other words, everything the ancients thought essential to an education – are being elbowed out by IT, business studies and other, newer 'vocational' subjects that might lead to a boring but reasonably well-paid job... but will they help young people to think critically and communicate eloquently – be better citizens?

That same evening, V emails me a link to an article that I think is designed to deter me from biting the hand that feeds you, as she puts it. A couple of years ago, five University of East London lecturers who'd repeatedly criticised their institution for its mercenary and bureaucratic ways found themselves threatened with redundancy. These academics were outstanding in their respective fields, so the decision could not have been based on academic or professional merit, so critics argued. One of the victims summed up the personal toll of such repression on her: 'I've gone through all the gamut of emotions: anger, stress, sadness. Like the others, I'm over 50, and we would be job-hunting in the middle of a pandemic.' Eventually, these lecturers were either reinstated or, if they had been sacked, compensated. But I bet they were more careful about what they said about the powers that be from then on.

# February 8th

An open day. I'm roped into joining a group of FE students on a tour of one of our halls of residence. Afterwards I have a coffee with P, the manager of the hall. If I thought that, as a lecturer, I was at the sharp end of manifold crises affecting our students, she can trump me. Over the last two years there have been three suicides in her hall alone. 'They shouldn't build these bloody things so high,' P jokes, inappropriately.

She's also dealing with more cases of harassment than ever. A female Chinese student came to her in tears because she had been sexually assaulted in the street at night. She didn't want to report it to the police because she was worried about questions being asked about her visa. P tried to assure her that all would be well, but the student was adamant. Her silence may have been about self-survival. Foreign students are often compelled to bend the law when it comes to supporting themselves. Legally, they can only work twenty hours a week, except this typically doesn't generate enough income to live on. Thus they have to find an employer who will give them extra hours on the sly, or do side hustles such as sex work. The extra money is badly needed, considering that on average they pay more than twice what domestic students pay in fees. Then there's the additional burden of shelling out to travel home for the holidays.

About ten years ago, Q, an Italian Erasmus student of mine, told me that the financial guidance the university offered to foreign students was patronising and poor in every other way too. She was unimpressed when someone explained to her and other new arrivals how to go shopping and save money in the UK. 'It was no different to going shopping and saving money in Italy,' she said. 'It was as if they thought we were five years old.' Perhaps the university's mentality is *once we've got them over here and the fees are being paid, we needn't do fuck all for them.* I stayed in touch with Q for a while after she graduated and she told me about her boyfriend, a Colombian, who, after graduating from another British university, got a job and was expected to effectively pay twice to use the NHS. Not only were National Insurance Contributions being taken out of his monthly salary, but every time he renewed his UK visa he had to pay an additional fee towards our rapidly rotting health service. 'This wouldn't be so bad if you could get to see a doctor within three months,' remarked Q.

Sometimes the pressures come from the student's country of origin. P says she was shocked when, a few years ago, the new intake of Chinese undergrads arrived at the hall accompanied by representatives of the Chinese embassy in London. The G-men made the students fill out forms that P later found out asked all sorts of questions about their political views. This was in the aftermath of the pro-democracy protests in Hong Kong.

# February 11th

As one of three colleagues who are still in the office at 7pm, I advocate going to the pub. We need it – two hours later we're still knocking it back when the barman announces the start of a pub quiz. We enter for a laugh.

About midway through, I notice the member of another team, a fiftyish woman with the bent physique of an Anglepoise lamp, surreptitiously checking her mobile phone. There is a big sign at the bar saying NO MOBILE PHONES ALLOWED DURING PUB QUIZ. In the break, one of my colleagues reports this misdemeanour to the barman, who promises to sanction the offender. Some way into the second half, Ms Anglepoise is still playing, which annoys my other colleague no end. 'Well if they're gonna cheat and get away with it...' he hisses. He goes to the toilet and magically returns with the correct answers to the last three questions of the quiz. When the scores are announced, we end up winning... by three points.

Moderately wrecked by now, I lumber up to the bar to spend our prize money. An old boy in a CAMRA T-shirt and a beard, piccalilli-hued from nicotine, edges up to me and says, 'So you lot are academics, aren't you?'

I say we are.

'Well that's cheating isn't it? Like an Olympic athlete entering a school sports day.'

'Don't follow you, mate.'

'You chaps spend a lot of time reading and studying, so you've got an advantage over ordinary punters like us. Not very fair, if you ask me.'

'Do you think we spend all our time reading about Ed fucking Sheeran's back catalogue?'

Piccalilli Beard winces and backs off. I don't blame him – that wasn't a very nice thing to say. But it does reflect my frustration about the daft ideas non-academics have about academia. Piccalilli Beard won't be the only one who fanatically believes that my job involves amassing trivial facts for an instrumental objective like winning a pub quiz. Little do they know that a typical academic has such a narrow field of expertise that they won't necessarily possess any more general knowledge than a floorer or florist. Indeed, they might have decidedly *less* general knowledge than such folks, given that cultivating a narrow field of expertise tends to eat into time that could otherwise be spent reading.

# February 12th

Next morning, I feel like my brains and innards have been thrown into a 3000-rounds-per-minute spin dryer. Thank Christ it's a Saturday. I focus on regaining my motor skills by lunchtime, when I'm due to meet some relatives.

Having chanted to myself on the way to the restaurant 'I will never drink again,' when I get to the restaurant I immediately order a Bloody Mary. This fortifies me for the barrage of questions I receive from the older members of my family. That some of them used to be teachers themselves – although not in HE – does not stop them from having had the same wrong-headed assumptions about my job for over a decade, no matter how often I try to correct them.

'How much teaching do you have at the moment?'

'About six hours a week.'

'Oooh lovely. So you've got time to relax.'

'No, because, as I've told you before, being an academic isn't like being a schoolteacher. Teaching is just one aspect of the job. I spend about a further 44 hours a week on admin and, if I'm lucky, research.'

'When do you finish then?'

'Finish what?'

'Finish teaching for the year? I used to look forward to that and the nice long holiday.'

'Technically in about May—'

'Lovely.'

'That doesn't mean I can just sit in a jacuzzi drinking Slippery Nipples until October.'

And so it goes on. I suppose I ought to have a sophisticated theory on how and why the public are so ignorant about academia, but I don't. All I can say is that their image isn't helped by us having been, at least since the 1970s, the whipping boys of the conservative media and politicians eager to score populist points. And if people aren't swayed by that then they might have been indoctrinated by pop culture – from kids' cartoons to videogames to Hollywood movies – being riddled with stereotypes of the mad, test-tube-juggling professor with ungovernable white hair who is about as closely connected to ordinary life as Danny Dyer is to 15th-century Florentine sculpture.

# February 16th

Though I'm starting to doubt the value of attending EIHR meetings and trying to persuade colleagues that actual things need to be done, I nonetheless agree to contribute to a Zoom meeting entitled 'Race in Our University: Hopes and Challenges.' The organiser tells me beforehand that this will be an open and candid forum where researchers can share their experiences of bigotry and microaggression.

Instead, colleagues – exclusively white ones – fall over each other to boast about metrics met and targets hit. And everyone is 'elated' about it.

'I am elated to report that, as Grand High Witch Doctor-in-Chief of Tolerance and Identity Deliverables, we have successfully built a 12-point EIHR plan into our latest policy concord.'

'I am elated to report that, as Vice Potentate of Equal Opportunity Opportunities, we have successfully made our graduate students aware of their EIHR responsibilities under the Race Equality Act 2010.'

'I am elated to report that....'

I click on the 'hand up' emoji several times but am ignored by this avalanche of cringeworthy self-congratulation. It's as if by not listening to people talk about problems, the problems will disappear.

# February 12th

First day on the picket line. There's about 30 of us. A rep tells me that only half of UCU members at our branch are striking. A fraction of that number are picketing. I'm tempted to ask why they are wasting their money on their dues. I talk to T, who says she's shocked that no one else in her department is here. Her department is politics.

It's cold but our hearts are warmed by horn honks in solidarity from taxi drivers and other motorists. Most impressively, we get a blast from a train departing the nearby station. The RMT are on strike today too.

An old boy joins us to hand out leaflets to passersby. This is the first day of his retirement from the uni and, very admirably, he has decided to spend it with us.

Another old boy wearing a corduroy blazer bristling with red poppies stops to wave a crooked finger at us. 'You're a disgrace! What about your students? What about this country?'

# February 13th

Day two on the picket line. With one exception, I haven't seen any colleague at the rank of reader or professor join us yet. I assume they've been leant on by management. Over the morning, a few managers pass us sheepishly.

I hear second-hand about a colleague who's been pressured by her AO to keep working, as the building she's based in doesn't have a picket line outside so no one would know she was scabbing. The lead resorted to emotional and moral blackmail: 'Our student feedback will be bad and that could lose us our jobs in the longer run.' This is as odious as it is dishonest – all the students I've spoken to overwhelmingly support our aims. They know that they too will benefit from better paid and mentally and physically healthier lecturers.

At the end of the picket at 2pm, we join a rally in the town centre. Other trades unionists and activists are there. I appreciate the vibe of unity. I bump into a former student, L, who is now a schoolteacher and striking with the National Education Union. There's a stirring sense of continuity about this.

# February 14th

I'm sad and single, so I spend Valentine's Day evening reviewing a couple of journal articles. The first is methodologically dubious and yields little insight. Its research question is, broadly speaking, 'are right-wing newspapers and websites in Canada generally critical of the Liberal Party government's arts policies?' I think I know the answer already. In an act of 'data-scraping,' the authors have fed 80-odd articles from aforesaid outlets into some analytical program.

What answer did the program give? Yes. The researchers didn't need to go through 80 articles to figure that out. But they did, according to a colleague, because media research has long been under fire for not being 'scientific' enough in its methods. What's the point, though, of using scientific methods to arrive at a truism?

The next article is based on interviews with 11 middle-aged people about what they think of the state of Britain since

Brexit. The researcher seems to take everything they say at face value. They go as far as to extrapolate a conclusion about 'national attitudes' based on... a football team's worth of people. Another problem is that people don't always say what they mean... especially if they're on their best behaviour because they're being asked things by a university professor. Would their answers be different if their interrogator was a binman? Or belonged to a different gender or ethnic identity? Probably.

There's a school of thought – psychoanalysis – that claims humans don't have much control over what they say because they're being driven by powerful subconscious urges. Psychoanalysts like Todd McGowan would argue that such urges underpin racism, ethnocentrism, nationalism and other attitudes relevant to voting Leave. Since these urges aren't rational, people will often provide limited, inconclusive and contradictory responses to questionnaires. The scholar I'm reviewing might have at least acknowledged these psychological conditions, given the plethora of folks who changed their mind about wanting to quit the EU almost as soon as they put their cross in the 'Leave' box.

He's part of a trend of academics looking at the world through simplistic positivist and empirical lenses. Such research often leads to dubious technocratic conclusions. Jonathan Dean has called out the centrist political scientist – nicknamed the 'Pol Prof' – who is hamstrung by a trust in inflexible 'predictive analytic models' that, despite all the bold claims made for their scientific robustness, fail to account for events from the 2008 economic crash to the rise of outlier politicians like Corbyn and Trump.

There are some obvious reasons for this theoretical naivety. As universities are increasingly directed by a 'business ontology', in how they are internally managed and through their interactions with commerce and the state, so the intellectual work happening inside them becomes more instrumentarian. The modern scholar amasses what Shoshana Zuboff calls 'totalities of data' on certain state- and corporate-sanctioned topics. These datasets may lead to seemingly progressive 'insights' into removing 'glass ceilings' for women entrepreneurs, tackling workplace discrimination and other aspects of liberal identity politics that are easily recuperable by companies keen to 'diversify' their workforce while continuing to exploit, pollute and kill. Other scholars gather data on consumer tastes, public opinion and mass-behaviour, which directly serve the marketing or advertising aims of business. Long-form academic reports on social, economic or foreign policy packed with statistics and methodological justifications are funded or commissioned by government departments eager to imbue their often controversial programmes with scholarly credibility. The epitome of this is what we might call the military-industrial-academic complex.

## February 16th

I catch a long-distance coach on a Saturday morning to go and see some relatives in another city. I overhear two men in the seats in front of me being – how shall we put it? – politely Islamophobic.

'The main issue is that the Koran is innately violent. When that's the basis of your culture then it's no wonder you end up with suicide bombers and the like.'

'Yeah, Islam should have gone through a Reformation like we had in Christianity. That might have chilled them all out a bit.'

The men guffaw like Beavis and Butthead.

'The problem is, Islam isn't a European religion. That's why they can't ever really integrate into *our* society.'

'They're not like us, are they? I mean the Blacks now, they're like us, they're Christian.'

'When you emigrate somewhere you *must* get with the programme. You've got to leave your sexism and homophobia behind. When Rachel and I go on holiday to Spain, we don't expect everyone to speak English and serve us Doom Bar.'

'And you can't bring your medieval legal system with you,' adds the other guy.

Then one asks the other, 'How's the dissertation marking going?' I realise that they are lecturers employed by the same university as me. I dread to think how many students they have inflicted this polite-sounding poison on.

# February 17th

Back on the picket line. I volunteer to hand out flyers explaining the reasons for the strike. It's good to see a cameraman and other media representatives. I'm relieved that the students I approach accept the flyers graciously. It would be nice if they supported us, but that's too much to ask at a relatively conservative institution like ours. They might also have been put off by draconian clampdowns on student militancy elsewhere. Recently, Sheffield University used private eyes to dig up dirt on students who organised an occupation to protest Sheffield's sweet deals with the arms trade. This covert action resulted in students being charged with 'misconduct,' even though one of the accused could prove they weren't anywhere near Sheffield University at the time of the occupation. Another of the indicted became suicidally depressed.

In 2019, during UCU strikes over the draining of staff pensions, the VC of Liverpool University warned that students who missed class would be officially recorded as such. Universities are required to monitor the attendance of foreign students, whose visas can be revoked for missing classes without permission. None of this makes good on HE's rhetoric of 'putting the student front and centre.' Other institutions tried to make staff liable for such consequences, especially if students tried to get their fees refunded. So keen was Coventry University to break the strike that it established a private subsidiary plus a brand new attached union, which effectively banned its staff from joining the UCU.

With half an hour to go before the end of the picket and the cold biting hard, a most unexpected thing happens – the VC steps out of his office and onto the picket line. At first we can't figure out whether he's going to join us or at least publicly address us. Instead, like a visiting member of the Royal Family, he shuffles up to individual picketers, shakes their hands and spouts some banalities about how both sides are working hard to come to a resolution. As with my other brushes with university authority, there's no appetite for delving into the issues. The last thing the highly visible CEO of a market-facing corporation wants is a disagreement – relayed by local TV news – that might tarnish the brand.

# February 19th

I have the same thoughts about a sinister announcement this afternoon by our university executive board that we are tightening up our already Orwellian policy against speech or actions that could 'bring the institution into disrepute.' I guess big organisations like us are reluctant to make anything but the blandest of public statements, since even the mildest controversy can go viral and nobble our market reach. In the succeeding email trail, I'm heartened that several colleagues are as worried about this as I am.

One asks whether bringing the university into disrepute is code for drawing the ire of other state institutions we're keen to crawl up the backsides of: parliament, the corporate media, the armed forces, pro-establishment think-tanks and so forth. Another colleague contrasts these newfound nerves about publicity with the tweets and Facebook posts put out by our senior managers and press officers in solidarity with the George Floyd and Sarah Everard murders, even though the movements – such as Black Lives Matter – that coalesced around these crimes called for defunding the police, reparations for slavery and for a free, independent Palestine: measures that would rile our business partners in the police force, government and arms industry.

In summer 2020, such posturing was slammed as 'tokenistic' by 300 BAME and white academics and students in an open letter to then-education secretary, Gavin Williamson. They argued that universities had 'failed to seriously engage with the systemic and structural nature of racism.'

The replies to these questions are so vacuously non-committal that I forgot about them long before I could write them down here.

# February 22nd

After receiving some disappointing responses to FOI requests – apparently being transparent about our investments would breach 'sensitivity' and 'confidentiality' – I google around for other dodgy dealings between HE and the world beyond. Surely even the most conservative uni bigwigs would baulk at a deranged throng of far-right, homophobic anti-abortionists infiltrating their campus? Not all, it would seem.

In 2019, a 'pro-life' student pressure group at Glasgow University was allowed to affiliate with that institution's Students' Representative Council. The group was funded by US Christian fundamentalist lobbying outfit ADF International, which opposes same-sex marriage and had allies in Donald Trump's administration.

Moreover, I find out about a network of professors, mostly based in elite institutions, who are members of the 'academic advisory council' of the Global Warming Policy Foundation. GWPF's arch-conservative credentials include being founded by the arch-climate change sceptic Nigel Lawson and donating £10,000 to Suella Braverman's Conservative Party leadership campaign in 2022. The GWPF's publishing arm has released a short monograph on the 'ethics' of climate change policy by Peter Lee, professor of applied ethics at Portsmouth University. The foreword was provided by former Durham University lecturer and ex-Bishop of Chester, Peter Forster. His questioning of what he terms 'global-warming alarmism' is of a piece with an ultra-conservative worldview; he has elsewhere asserted that gay people can 'reorientate themselves,' for example.

In the evening, E phones me. He's upset about a 'bad review' he's received on some website that allows students to give their lecturers ratings out of five. He's been called 'dull' and 'annoying' and been slammed for 'spreading lefty propaganda.' I tell him not to worry about it. It's just one opinion that almost nobody will read anyway.

'That review has already had 300 upvotes,' E sighs.

'Ah. That's not many in the grand scheme of all the people on the internet,' I try to reassure him.

'I put my life and soul into my teaching,' sighs E. 'I don't think the kids understand that.'

'Of course they do. That's just one student who's moaning, probably because it's a way of covering their own arse over not having turned up all year.'

'If so, that could be anyone. *Most* of them haven't turned up all year.'

I'm trying to put a brave face on it but, I admit, had I received such a stinker, I'd be as glum as he is.

'Can't help but think there's something fishy about it,' E adds. 'I never broach politics in class so how do they reckon I'm a raging lefty? Also, the review was suspiciously well written. Nobody on that module is *that* articulate. It was like they'd been helped by some professional.' With the caveat of 'I'm not paranoid but...' E goes on to tell me about a well-funded new cell operating in the UK – again of American provenance – that is helping students to push back against what it sees as the 'woke' conquest of campuses.

'I think they'll find their job has already been done for them by the Kingdom of Saudi Arabia and Raytheon UK,' I quip.

'That may be so but these tossers must have missed that meeting.' E emails me a link to an article that alleges this group employs several full-time staff, used to be run by the son of a Tory Party treasurer and has branches in eight British universities. The group's UK launch featured leading members of the Taxpayers' Alliance, Leave Means Leave and the Leave.EU campaign. Also in attendance were an online 'pick-up artist' and writers for conspiracy theory websites with a line in Islamophobia and anti-semitism.

When I come to the end of the article, I go back over it to check that it is indeed an exposé... and not a guest wish-list for our VC's fantasy dinner party.

# February 25th

I meet up with an old mate from my undergraduate days. He didn't go into academia, so is disturbed by my revelations about what it's like today. When I'm done whingeing, he scratches his head and says, 'Wasn't it beginning to get like that when we were students? I'm sure the first I ever heard of phrases like "service provider" was at university. And I remember the VC calling our institution "a global brand."'

My memory isn't as good as his, but I think he's right. The university we attended was at the forefront of HE commercialisation. Maybe what happened there in the 1990s took a couple of decades to happen in the institution where I work now.

'I remember us taking the mick when we read about "professional development" in some brochure,' says my mate.

'That's right. And I remember saying to W, "Do you have any idea of what job you'll get after graduation?"'

'And he said, "What a disgraceful question."'

The neoliberal writing was on the wall in other ways, too. In our first year the university refectory was run directly by the college, heavily subsidised and therefore cheap. The middle-aged female staff treated us students with respect and an almost maternal affection. It was probably to do with my hormones, but the 19-year-old me enjoyed a stranger addressing me as 'love,' 'darling' or 'babe.' The agreeable atmosphere was short-lived. By the second year the refectory had been annexed by a private franchise which upped the prices beyond our budget and employed a cadre of overworked and underpaid depressives who barely spoke. Now I bet there isn't a single university-run refectory anywhere in Britain.

My mate asks me about teaching. I say it's difficult to enthuse the kids.

'I have to admit,' he says, 'that I wasn't very enthusiastic myself. The syllabus was basically a re-tread of one of my A-Levels, taught by lecturers who were either bumbling to the point of incomprehensibility or so utterly lacking in charisma and expression that they'd be better suited to addressing a pipework conference in Eastbourne.'

'Often they *were* somewhere else,' I added. 'On the *Today* programme or at a conference in a suspiciously hot and exotic country.'

My mate blushes. 'Sorry, I didn't mean to imply that you're like any of those lecturers and that's why you can't enthuse the kids.'

'No offence taken. At least I'm better than Dr Z. Remember him?'

'How could I forget? He was supposed to be my personal tutor and my first and only meeting with him lasted about 90 seconds.'

He was my tutor, too, and I had the same experience. When I entered Dr Z's office, he leaned forward over his desk and squinted at me as if he had just discovered some brand new species. I guessed he didn't come across students very often.

'Hello,' I said, waving at him, hoping he would snap out of it.

Dr Z pointed to a chair. Each time I spoke, he would slide his hand up the front of his blazer to his ear and stick his index finger inside it, or scratch the lobe with his little finger. I had the impression that he was sending me this subliminal message: 'I hate you and I don't want to listen to you.'

Any chance of ever warming to him evaporated when I saw that his shelves were lined with books by Henry Kissinger. I'd just read a damning article by Christopher Hitchens accusing Kissinger of supporting yahoo despots like General Pinochet and of committing war crimes in Vietnam and Cambodia. I wondered what earlier, more radical generations of students would have made of Dr Z's 'research interests.'

'But the worst one,' says my mate, 'was Dr K. What the hell happened to him if what I read in the news about godless commies invading universities is true?'

'That isn't true, by the way. If Dr K was hired by our place he'd find plenty of bigots to hang out with, but would have to dial his attitudes down in front of students.'

Dr K taught me on a unit about the connections between race and sex in colonial history, and I learned precisely one thing from him that whole term: his oddball theory of homosexuality. According to him, some little boys form strong relationships with their uncles, and this makes them gay later in life. In the finest traditions of academic rigour, Dr K didn't offer any evidence for his claim other than anecdotes about his own family. Indeed, when I found out later that Dr K was gay, it was possible that his theory might have applied to just one single case: his own. What might have been dismissed as slightly gauche eccentricity was cast into a more sinister light by Dr K's well-known affiliations with far-right organisations.

# February 26th

A seminar discussion strays into how values have changed over time. Though this isn't the topic I'd planned, I want to see if the digression proves enlightening. A female student who wears a woollen beanie hat, whatever the weather, says that young people today have no discipline. 'My granddad did national service and it made him a good citizen. We should bring it back.' Has anyone expressed a view like this since circa 1955?

'I see,' I reply. 'How do others feel about that?' I scan the rows of faces. A girl with a peace-sign sticker on her laptop grimaces. I assume the general silence to mean they disagree.

Another student says they watched a documentary on a streaming site about the fashion industry in the 2000s. They were shocked by revelations of sexual misconduct. 'I guess it was okay in the noughties, though,' they conclude.

'That sort of thing *wasn't* okay in the noughties.' I feel oddly protective about an era that I lived through – and that few others in this room did.

'There was less tolerance then, wasn't there?' asks another student.

'Perhaps.' I decide to share memories of kids trading insults like 'queer' and 'gaylord' when I was at school, and of teachers telling naff jokes about 'dodgy' Irish builders. It wasn't much better at university in the era of the 'New Lad.' White kids aspiring to be Black would call women 'bitches.' Males generally talked openly about wanking and porn.

For the generation before mine, I continue, it wasn't just the Irish on the end of racist epithets. When my parents came of age in the permissive 1960s, women were still expected to clean the communes and boil the lentils. A hundred years before that, women couldn't vote or go to university. Had they been allowed to study for a science degree in those days they would have been taught that pecking orders of race and gender were 'natural' and 'biological.' At the top of these ladders were posh white men with ridiculous facial hair.

By the time I'm finished saying all this, it's not just the peacenik who's grimacing. I may have triggered them...

# February 27th

N stays back after class to have a word with me. She stands out from her peers in several ways. Like what were called goths in my youth, she wears deep eye shadow, has various piercings across her face and dons Victorian-style stockings and torn dresses. She's also easily the brightest in the class, versed in public speaking and evidently well-read. I guess from her accent and her confident bearing she is privately educated, which would put her in a tiny minority round here.

'I feel... I feel as though this class isn't a safe space for me,' she says.

'I'm very sorry to hear that. How can I help to make it safer for you?'

'It's... certain people. You must have noticed.'

'Sorry, I'm not following you.'

'The way that some people look at me. When I'm talking. They look annoyed with me.'

'I haven't noticed. Are you sure—'

'I'm not being paranoid!' she snaps.

'Of course not.'

'It's a *kind* of bullying.'

'Right. Can you tell me who the offenders are?'

'No, because then they'll be even more horrible to me.'

'Right. The problem is, it's quite difficult to resolve an issue like this if I don't know who the culprits are. It's also hard to prove whether someone gave a *certain* look, as I'm sure you'll understand. Has anyone said anything to you that could be construed as bullying?'

She thinks about it, sucks on the metal bolt through her lower lip. 'I've been interrupted by one of the culprits. When I was in mid-flow. I think that's bullying.'

'Again, I can't say I've noticed. I always try to be scrupulously fair about giving all my students the opportunity to speak without interruption. It's very important to me as a teacher.'

I'm about to conclude that N is over-sensitive and make my excuses, when she grows more voluble. She tells me about her girlfriend who likes to instigate ferocious arguments about the merits of comic books and internet memes. While N's partner seems unfazed afterwards, N takes it badly. She has tried to confront her partner about what is *really* bugging her, as it seems ludicrous to get so exercised over the *oeuvre* of Neil Gaiman. However, her partner denies that she is bothered about anything other than Neil Gaiman. N reckons she's displacing some serious issues with their relationship. I thought this kind of classic English self-repression was more typical of men than women, but then we live in a more gender-equal society nowadays.

I'm reminded of an undergraduate acquaintance I had, whom we'll call V. V was the brightest of anyone I knew at uni. He'd read everything. I once loaned him a Margaret Atwood novel which he read in a few hours and was able to discuss in extraordinary detail, quoting long passages verbatim. This bespoke geniuses like Oscar Wilde who, apparently when he was a student, could read a text overnight and memorise vast chunks of it. Unlike Mr Wilde, V had no social skills whatsoever. He would shout over people he disagreed with and quickly personalise an argument about an abstract idea.

He was particularly hostile to women. One evening at the union bar, I was chatting up a female PhD student and he scuppered it by opining, 'You joined the LibDems – that's pretty fucking stupid, isn't it?' He then launched into a very cogent but also very angry leftist critique of liberal ideology. The woman stormed out of the bar. Later on, V had the cheek to say to me that *she* was a bit aggressive but that he would forgive her that because it was part of her sex appeal. Like a badly behaved child, you couldn't take him anywhere for fear he would upset everyone else present.

Until then I had always assumed a short temper was the product of insecurity, especially about one's intellect. But he had nothing to worry about on that score. In his formative years perhaps his parents had given him enough books but not enough love. Maybe they'd got him reading and writing aged two but had left him alone screaming in his cot too often.

After he had alienated enough of our peers, I had a word with him about his conduct. We'd gathered one evening in another student's room in our hall of residence to get stoned and play Playstation. Before long, V had picked a verbal fight with someone about existentialism – or something like that – and I took this as my cue.

I looked him in the eye and said, 'What are you doing?'

He shrugged. 'Talking. Debating.'

'No, you're dominating. And you're being obnoxious about it. You *have to* win the argument, however trivial it is. But it's a hollow victory because you never convince anyone, you just shout them down. You always assume that nobody else knows anything. I mean, what's the point?'

'Of what?'

'Of what you're doing now.'

'I'm trying to tell you the truth about Jean-Paul Sartre.'

'Bullshit. This has nothing to do with Jean-Paul Sartre. This is to do with you. You're just using Jean-Paul Sartre as a stick to beat others with.'

His features pinched with hurt.

'When you bully and shout, people are not likely to agree with the point you are making. It doesn't work. If you really cared about persuading people you'd listen to what they have to say and respond to it. You have incredible knowledge and intelligence but you don't know basic manners. You call yourself a socialist but you espouse your socialism in this nasty way. You talk in abstract terms about egalitarianism but you don't treat people in an egalitarian way. Can't you see that? If the revolution ever happens, you'd be the last person I'd want leading it.'

'The point I'm making about Sartre—'

'Fuck Sartre!' I looked over at our peers. They were all staring gloomily at the carpet. What happened to them backing me up? Now this was looking like me bullying *him*. Now I looked like the aggressor with some personal hang-up about V.

I avoided him from then on. Gradually, others did the same.

Some years later, my workplace has more than its fair share of those suffering from V-like conditions. They too ought to get to know themselves before being unleashed on others.

# February 30th

Up at insanity o'clock to talk to the admin manager of the foreign university. She's young and very attractive. Is this a strategy on the part of her institution? A heterosexual man of a certain age – i.e., we who dominate Western academia still – might be beguiled into discarding his reservations or not asking hard questions.

She asks me about my current salary, my expected remuneration and, to be honest, a load of other information that I already provided in the application form. I realise that rituals with no practical purpose are not the preserve of the Western academy.

She then reads out a list of administrative information such as start and end dates of the academic year – which I already know because it's on the institution's website – and advises me that I should open a local bank account if I do take up the post.

# March 5th

It's one of life's many contradictions that an institution like ours, which purports to be frantic about its market survival, wouldn't know what publicity was if it leapt out and gave it a big fat sloppy kiss on the lips. I have this thought while I navigate our university website, squinting at the gaudy clash of primary colours and the babyish hieroglyphics – test tube denoting research, smiley face signifying student welfare, pen and notepad leading to a contact details page etc – that look to have come from a Clip Art folder circa 1985. I have the fierce conviction that a team of witless monkeys constructed this site for about £25.

Betwixt the bromides – 'own your future', 'unlock your potential', 'train to be a thought leader' – there's info on our gym, swimming pool, football and cricket teams, parking spaces, where to get food on campus, digital hubs and 'touch-down spaces'. However – and call me Professor Pernickety – there isn't a single mention of education until you've scrolled through all the above. If a university has one USP, surely it's education. The gym may be good, but can it – or should it – compete with all the gyms that are out there already? And the only places to buy food on campus make the local burger van look like the Savoy Grille.

At Newcastle University, Ozzie, an elderly cat who strolls around the campus, has more followers on Instagram than the VC of that same uni does on Twitter.

# March 8th

I'm invited to speak at a 'decolonising territories and discourses' meeting. I assume someone somewhere with some power has seen the word 'decolonial' near my name on our intranet. I explain to the audience of eight that, behind all the hot air, HE is involved in anything but decolonisation, what with its buddying up with Global South-bashing armies and weapons dealers. Some of the younger attendees are nodding away, the older ones in charge of the meeting are not. An ancient emeritus professor scowls at me for a minute before falling asleep. I make a dig about this at the end of my talk: 'If everyone's still awake after that, shall we have some questions?'

I'm hoping for a debate about the issues I've raised. But rather than responding to my arguments head-on, Emeritus tries to infer that my talk is somehow inappropriate. 'It isn't clear to me what contributions you are making to the academic knowledge about decolonisation,' he says.

I'm tempted to say that it isn't clear to him because he was dozing through my talk. Instead, I claim that there can be no more urgent academic task than defining what is meant by decolonisation. If there is ambiguity about the very meaning of the term then how can we proceed in a rigorous or coherent way? I add in a cliché for good measure: 'It's like trying to run before you've learned to walk.' That we don't yet have a consistent definition, I continue, might explain the pretzel logic of an academic tweeting in favour of refugees in the morning... and then sharing an advert for CIA-sponsored research fellowships in the afternoon... and failing to see how the second phenomenon contributes to the first.

I realise this was a faux pas when I spot other faces in the room deflating. Later, when these faces introduce themselves as cybersecurity and counter-terrorism experts, it dawns on me that they are exactly the types who would apply for CIA-sponsored research fellowships.

A reader in law says, 'What sorts of academic conclusions or solutions have you arrived at?'

I'm tempted to lean over and check whether cloth has been jammed in his ears for the last 40 minutes. Rather, I mention some modest proposals based on what other unis have already done: divestment from dodgy business partners, proper drives to recruit BAME staff etc.

'I said *academic* solutions.'

I think I see what he's getting at: I've committed the cardinal sin of mixing politics with academic research. It'd be nice if he had the courage to say so. 'Decolonisation is surely inherently political,' I reply. 'Every serious scholar in this field – from Fanon to Said – saw nothing but continuity between their intellectual endeavours and their political commitments.' The blank expressions persuade me that these highly paid and somewhat respected academics aren't hip to the key scholars in the field. So what do they spend their working days doing?

Although I've almost certainly lost this crowd already, I add, for good measure:

'And of course, the assertion that academic research should be apolitical is itself a highly political one.'

None of the young 'uns who were nodding earlier speak up in my defence. Is this because they are PhD students reluctant to publicly gainsay their supervisors or other superiors on whom they depend in various ways?

As another senior colleague closes the meeting, I notice Emeritus rolling his vast, skullular eyes.

These jokers are not interested in addressing the systemic and structural causes of racism and imperialism. For them, it's a matter of image and representation, rather than life and death – so nothing will change.

The more I think about these colleagues in the decolonising group, the surer I am that their faux progressivism isn't just inadequate for solving the problems our university faces. Worse than that, their rhetoric of human rights and decolonisation is in fact *exacerbating* all the problems it claims to want to solve. Behind their smokescreen of fine talk, violence, repression and censorship continues without proper scrutiny or accountability. It's a bit like someone who secretly goes around robbing old grannies while spending the rest of their time extolling the virtues of old grannies, thereby distracting anyone concerned about how and why all these old grannies keep getting mugged.

# March 14th

Although it's not my field, I attend a public talk given by the commissioning editor of a trade publisher that specialises in autobiography. Our dean of research has arranged this to make our institution look more 'industry facing.' He also hopes that we academics will pitch a book to this editor that a fair number of people might (a) want to read and (b) pay money for.

Though the editor is a good speaker, I'm not sold on the travel-inflected memoirs she's keen on. From what she says, it appears that every such book these days begins with an existential crisis. It takes as long as middle age for a hedge fund manager to realise that he is a parasitical bastard who might do less damage to society by trekking around Cumbria ogling bluetits. A 30-year-old woman with the 'perfect' education, the 'perfect' job and the 'perfect' apartment in New York City decides that the word 'perfect' as defined by contemporary, middle-class America is actually quite an unsavoury condition to find yourself in, and so hops on the first plane to somewhere in the Global South, runs amok in a rainforest or desert, and comes home with 270 pages of homilies about fortitude, independence and sympathy for brown people considerably poorer than her. Then there's the daredevil who, due to some unresolved personal trauma caused by childhood tragedy or involvement in a Middle Eastern war, sets off on a hair-raisingly hazardous journey like swimming straitjacketed up the Congo River or unicycling stark naked across North Korea. Pretty much the sole narrative object of such 'adventure travel' books is raising money for charity, which fits the logic of our neoliberal world of intense competition and bankrupted human services.

# March 16th

At the less ungodly hour of 6am UK time, I rise and deliver by Zoom a presentation to the foreign university about my teaching. I make it simple and entry-level, focusing on how I would teach the kids to write in basic style. I notice that all the bigwigs around the table are native to that country – or look native to that country – save one who looks Western.

In the discussion afterwards, one of the panellists says my presentation was 'too advanced' for their students. If I'd simplified it any more, I'd have descended to kindergarten lows. Then, in a 'good cop-bad cop' dynamic someone else says, 'We enjoyed your talk and are impressed with the materials you have submitted. We are therefore going to recommend your hiring to the executive level of the university. If this is approved – which we expect it to be – we can make you a formal offer.'

'That's good news, thank you,' I say. 'But I just have a few questions about the nature of the job, particularly the split between teaching and research and the use of the discretionary budget. If I'm going to make this very big career change – moving to a foreign country, adapting to a new culture – I need to know that it's going to help me to become a more research-oriented academic.'

The gorgeous admin manager says she will set up a meeting with another professor to discuss this.

'With respect,' I say, 'we've had a lot of meetings already and they do always take place at inconvenient times for me. Is there any chance someone could just provide me the answers to my questions by email?'

The panellists rubberneck one another with barely repressed fury.

# March 20th

Vacuous ritual number 42,345. Our HoD sends round his yearly email requesting staff to take on roles relating to course leadership, ethics committees and timetabling. These emails are sent every year and every year almost nobody responds. Colleagues are dubious about taking on unpaid extra work. An organisation that prides itself on its corporate guile might by now have grasped the concept of financial incentivisation.

The upshot is that the few who do volunteer for these jobs are completely unsuitable. Some will volunteer because they don't already do enough teaching or research... which means they don't know much about teaching or research... which means they shouldn't be entrusted with making decisions about teaching or research. Meanwhile, megalomaniacs and narcissists will spy an opportunity to lord it over others and gain the respect they've been missing since their childhood.

Into this category would go a strikingly unpleasant colleague called J, who has the doughnut midriff of almost every middle-aged male lecturer round here. While I don't work directly with him, I've heard enough about his shenanigans that I'm flabbergasted as to why he is allowed within a mile radius of a centre of higher learning, let alone employed in one. Despite being a grown man, he doesn't realise how unappealing it is to jabber on about how great he is at his job. 'I rule' and 'I'm smashing it' are two of his catchphrases. People who flaunt it don't often have it, although there are some exceptions like Muhammad Ali. J is an unapologetic grade-inflator, awarding firsts to submissions that are as coherent as Shane MacGowan after a four-day bender. This isn't as crude as his other strategies for sucking up to students. He tries – and fails – to make out he's 'one of them' by using the terms of reference of someone who not only hates students, but hasn't met one for 30-odd years. The result makes David Brent look erudite.

J's induction week spiel involves lines like, 'I know you're all gonna be out on the piss every night this week and gorging yourselves on takeaways, but do try and look after yourselves, yeah?' If you recall the excruciating expression on the face of Dr Birx, the White House Coronovarius response coordinator, when she was asked by Donald Trump in 2020 whether injections of disinfectant could cure Covid, I bet she felt only half as embarrassed as I did when I witnessed J extolling the virtues of sausage rolls... to a room full of students, at least two of whom were Muslim.

J likes to curry favour with students by dishing out chocolate biscuits in class, announcing to them 'you are my children.' The student feedback implies that his 'children' dislike being infantilised. 'He tries too hard,' is a common gripe. 'He's a bit weird.' And rightly so – you'd have to be conspicuously dense to be taken in by such shameless arse-kissing. It is no puzzle, then, why several senior managers are fans of J.

Like Monty Python's cigar-chomping tycoons romanticising their humble beginnings, J complains that he has spent most of his career working sweatshop hours for minimum wage on a temporary contract, even though for some years he has had a permanent, full-time post paying £50,000 a year.

Now J plans to take on a leadership role that will allow him to be even more of an un-collegiate wanker than he was before. His immediate colleagues are organising to stop this happening. It's probably unethical to gossip with those same colleagues about this conflict, but it's also quite amusing, so that's what I spend the afternoon doing.

I learn that J's inferiority complex may be driven by *actual* inferiority. He has published very little, and what little he has published is in low-impact journals or on his personal blog and far-from-academic websites, which are not peer-reviewed. His colleagues would forgive these faults if he was amiable, but he isn't so they're going to protest to the HoD about his promotion. Almost certainly J *does* care about his academic weaknesses and it probably drives his compulsion to undermine others.

Another colleague opposed to J's promotion tells me, 'You know when a serial killer or some other hideous criminal is finally caught, their friends and neighbours are interviewed in the media and they always say, "He was such a quiet person – I had no idea he would have done something so terrible"? Well, in J's case if they did find severed heads in his fridge, it wouldn't surprise me at all.'

I giggle, expecting my colleague to follow suit, but he looks serious.

'Thank God it's relatively hard to access semi-automatic firearms,' he continues, 'or J would have charged into the office and slaughtered us all already. I bet you it's at least crossed his mind that if all his colleagues are dead then they won't be able to silently judge his research credentials and ability to do his job.'

# April 2nd

With the Easter break almost upon us, I have a tutorial with an MA student whose essay on the class divide among students is highly accomplished and probably publishable. Student fees, he argues, were introduced in 1998 to putatively fund broader curricula offered by universities, which would in turn attract poorer candidates into HE, which would in turn improve social mobility across Britain. But the direct reverse happened: there was a dive in applications post-'98 and the long-term result is today only about 10 per cent of the most disadvantaged kids in society attend university, according to UCAS's own figures. If, like my student, you are one of the lucky few to get into university, once you're there you don't feel so lucky next to your middle-class peers. While they can call on the Bank of Mum and Dad to top up their loans, chances are your parents are on benefits, or doing minimum wage labour, so can't spare any cash. You have to do two jobs – in addition to studying – just to make ends meet. The better-off students have the luxury of partying and neglecting their studies because, even if they get a rubbish degree, they'll probably be financially secure in the long run due to familial affluence and the right connections in the job market. On the other hand, you'll have to work extra hard to get a good degree – and even then you're not assured of security afterwards, given the surfeit of similarly qualified people competing for the same posts.

In addition, my student has established, through diligent research, that working-class families have a cultural aversion to letting their kids get into heaps of debt over three years, when they might as well start working and earning, as it's a hard, expensive life ahead. I've been there myself. By the time I graduated in my early twenties – and was totally skint – I had friends who had bought their own homes and could afford to start a family, as they'd gone and got a job in a bank or on a building site.

# April 25th

B, a pony-tailed metaller, meets me in the refectory. He's livid about failing a third-year unit despite not attending a single class all year. 'It's not fair,' he moans. 'I worked really hard on this.'

I know that's false because one of B's peers snitched to me. An hour before the deadline, B was in the IT suite, still writing his submissions. Rather than mention this, I speculate that his turning up to only one out of 24 classes might have led to his sorry grade.

'I had good reasons,' he says. He starts ticking off each class with his fingers. 'So weeks one to three, I was at a wedding.'

'That's a long wedding,' I reply.

'Erm, it was one of them Indian ones. My mate's Indian, yeah?'

'What about all the other weeks?'

'My uncle – yeah my uncle – died in week four. Yeah that's it, my uncle. Week four.'

'My deepest condolences.' I try my damnedest to repress a giggle. Judging from his smirk, so does he.

'Then... where are we?' B asks.

'Week five.'

'England were playing at Wembley. You've got to let me have that!'

'Our class is 9–11am,' I remind him – or perhaps this is the first he's heard of it. 'Weekday matches are normally in the evening, no?'

And so it goes on like that. We both know it's a charade but I guess he feels like he has to at least try to defend himself, even if he's about as convincing as Prince Andrew's *Newsnight* interview. To be fair, he's no worse than anyone else at this university, colleagues included.

## May 7th

I receive an email from the student who, back in January, accused several colleagues and I of racial discrimination. This message is full of praise about what an inspiring and caring lecturer I have been. The final line asks if I will write them a job reference. They can go and do something obscene to themselves.

## May 9th

I'm just leaving the office when I bump into F, a 60-something-year-old colleague who I thought had retired at least a year ago. 'Where... have you... been?' I blurt.

'On sick leave for the last few months.'

I'm sure it's been longer than that.

F twigs my confusion and says, 'I had another period off last year, so I've not been in here much.'

This reminds me that, under the terms of our contracts, we lecturers can get six months' sick leave on full pay. Any longer than that and this drops down to half-pay. I'm assuming F did the smart thing and took two non-consecutive periods of leave.

A colleague shuffles past us. 'Congratulations, F, on making reader this time. And on your new monograph.'

Clearly there aren't rules against working towards promotion and writing books... while you are 'off sick.' Despite my cynicism, I don't necessarily blame anyone for taking this option. Lecturers are increasingly so swamped with admin we seldom get any time to conduct the research we're told is essential to our existence. It may also be true that, if one is off with mental distress, a creative activity such as writing a book might be good therapy.

It might also be better than persevering with your normal work duties, if they are making you psychologically sick. On occasion, this can be fatal. In 2018, Malcolm Anderson, a senior lecturer in accountancy, jumped from the roof of the building at Cardiff University where he worked. Anderson was a perfectionist who would go above and beyond the call of duty by responding to student emails in the dead of night, and often worked evenings and weekends. At time of his death in February 2018, he was in the middle of marking 418 exam papers and preparing for lectures.

Professor Stefan Grimm took his own life in 2014 after he felt under pressure from Imperial College to bring in tens of thousands of pounds' worth of research income. In an email he scheduled to be delivered to collagues after his death, the toxicology professor wrote: 'This is not a university anymore but a business with [a] very few up in the hierarchy... profiteering [while] the rest of us are milked for money, be it professors for their grant income or students who pay 100 pounds just to extend their write-up status.' Imperial expressed its sadness at the 'tragic loss' but denied that it had placed the review or given him notice that he was losing his job.

While we're fortunate not to have had a staff suicide at our institution, certain colleagues are less than mentally fit for work. One early morning last year in our open-plan office, an older and indecorous reader speculated that 70 per cent of our colleagues were 'on the happy pills' as he put it. A younger, newer lecturer arrived at their desk, and my older colleague asked them, 'You're on 'em too and all, aren't you?' I've never seen someone look so embarrassed.

# May 10th

I catch up with two ex-students who were members of what I recall as a golden generation of enthusiastic, courteous and conscientious kids. Such qualities feel like they belong to an ancient era – in fact, these guys graduated in the midst of the Coronavirus pandemic. They're doing well now. One is about to work overseas in academia, the other has a mid-level gig in publishing. Despite Covid, they tell me they got a lot out of the course and that I was the best teacher they ever had.

They ask me how my current bunch are. They cannot believe the nosedives in attendance and morale in just a few years. 'Take me with you,' I ask the one who's moving abroad for an academic role.

# May 13th

I'm invited to meet my HoD and AO to discuss a delicate and unprecedented matter. On social media someone has been posting messages critical of our department and the institution. Our hunch is that it's a current student – certainly the rhetoric is that of a dissatisfied customer. While it wins me no friends, I venture that, since we treat students as customers, is it wholly unexpected that they might behave like customers?

'Even so, we are where we are,' says my HoD. 'And we need to do some firefighting on this, *right now*.'

I glance over to the fire extinguisher clamped to the wall before realising this is just another zombie figure of speech.

It turns out that the troll has some IT acumen. As soon as they are blocked or muted from the university's various accounts, they respawn like a videogame hero under a new handle to torment us another day.

Nerdy young C, who wears dungarees and works in our digital marketing department, says this is tricky, since her team has an obligation to answer queries from the public. If this team simply bans anyone who disagrees with the university line, we'll be seen to be repressive or draconian.

My own (unspoken) take on this is that the university is indeed repressive and draconian – and this is patent to most who work for it – but I guess apparatchiks like C must ensure that the public – potential customers, partners, stakeholders – don't find this out.

C shows us on her tablet a collage of the troll's barbs. The first is correct in spirit if not in detail:

FFS you wasted £10 million on rubbish new emblem looks like swastika. Your top brass Giles Coren-smug about it. FFS it's taxpayers & feepayers $$!

I try not to laugh at 'Giles Coren-smug.' It's a good line.

Poor C shows us her response: Thank you for your comment, RebeloftheMiddle99. Let us clarify a few things. Creating the emblem didn't cost £10 million. In fact, £2 million – of funds raised privately, not from the taxpayer – were spent on adding the new emblem to our signage, letterheads and other materials. We don't feel that the emblem looks like a swastika and our senior management are pleased rather than smug about the success of the project.

The troll then pasted a link to a blog called *Will the Whistleblower*. This, C surmises, is written by a disgruntled ex-university employee for whom taking revenge on his former bosses trumps tiny trifles such as backing up his provocative statements with evidence.

'When I checked Will's post,' says C, 'I found that none of the claims about the £10 million, the managerial smugness or whether the emblem resembles a swastika – which is surely subjective anyway – are embedded with supporting links. The post is also riddled with spelling, grammar and punctuation mistakes.'

My AO chimes in. 'If we're dealing with a fantasist who only makes himself look stupid by sharing fake news, what are we worried about?'

'It doesn't matter whether it's fake or not,' says our HoD. 'The point is, it's posted. There. In the public domain. Even if it had been taken down within five minutes, untold numbers would have seen it and believed it—'

'—Because they don't care about facts either?' I interject.

'Precisely,' sighs our HoD.

Sheepishly, C says, 'I naively thought that countering unreliable evidence with reliable evidence would sort this out, so I pasted a link to our press office's article about the re-branding which backed me up and not RebeloftheMiddle99.'

Propaganda! was RebeloftheMiddle99's predictable reply. Article by uni press office bound to try make uni look good! Not neutral like my source!

Rest assured, typed T, our press officers are trained journalists who use dependable sources and fact-check all their articles before publication.

She then shows us a link to another, supposedly more objective article on the website of the local newspaper. Unfortunately, that's no paragon of accuracy either – it has next to no budget to hire reporters, find trustworthy sources or employ fact-checkers. Masses of complaints against it have been upheld by IPSO.

`Rubbish`, wrote RebeloftheMiddle99. `U can't even spell. Look at this.`

'He had us there,' says C, 'with a link to one of our stories that was written by an intern... who turned out to be severely dyslexic.'

My AO clasps their hands together. 'Alright, I think we get it, C. Let's talk to this student face-to-face, get to the root of their discontent.'

'The snag with that,' replies C, 'is that we're not sure if this is a current student. Nor do we know if this is one person acting alone. There have been so many different handles and accounts trolling us these past three months that my team suspects there's a group at work. Some of the members may not even be affiliated with the uni.'

'Beam me up, Scotty,' says the HoD.

# May 17th

I seem to have *been volunteered* to solve the troll problem, so meet again just with C. She's done some more investigating of RebeloftheMiddle99's digital footprint. In many ways, his – and I think it is reasonable to assume this is a he – behaviour is typical of anyone who dives down the rabbit hole of social media 'activism' and can't burrow their way out. The only surprise is that the online groups RebeloftheMiddle99 lurks in are not the rabid ones you'd imagine. The Social Liberal Forum, Unite to Remain, Labour First – these are all centrist outfits.

From the materials C shows me, it appears that he, like so many others, has succumbed to that peculiar carrot-and-stick reward system that drives social media, and that countless studies have shown to be as addicting as alcohol and nicotine. In hot pursuit of a dopamine buzz, he has read the first two lines of thousands of posts by people he has never met and responded in a way that implies that our culture has reduced the complex rainbow of human emotions to several fucking stupid little cartoon faces.

When we start looking at what RebeloftheMiddle99 has written, rather than merely emoji'd, there's no consistent moral or political outlook. He aims to please different factions at different times, changing his opinion depending on who he's engaging with at the time. Often this manifests itself in crowd-pleasing sentiments that are so bland and truistic that almost no one would disagree. `That Donald Trump, he's a narcissistic criminal isn't he? Or Boris Johnson u are such a liar shame on u.` On the other hand, though, when RebeloftheMiddle99 does commit to a position – for the length of a thread – he does so with such vitriol that he can't expect to win anyone over to his cause. Colourful adjectives and ad hominems launched at Brexiteers and left-of-Labour Party figures demonstrate that being a twat online is not exclusive to any ideology. The more I read of this stuff, the more I doubt that RebeloftheMiddle99 has any interest in persuading people. The point might be to superficially look like he is 'winning' or 'clever' or something like that, since the people RebeloftheMiddle99 picks fights with are fairly well-known journalists and academics. Like a certain colleague discussed above, I suspect RebeloftheMiddle99 is insecure in the company of whom he sees, grudgingly, as 'real' writers or intellectuals.

Devoted to the online convention of 'LWS' ('Last Word Syndrome'), RebeloftheMiddle99 always tries to be the last to post in an online spat. I notice the deployment of cheeky techniques such as, when he senses he is 'losing' the argument, writing, `Look mate, I can't spend more time on this as got proper work to do`. Usually the wheeze works because his adversaries have (a) only so much patience or (b) have proper work to do themselves, so they let it slide and let him have the last word.

Other familiar howlers are all over the screenshots C has made. Some posts show RebeloftheMiddle99 repeatedly agreeing with his antagonist despite the substance of the post evidently not. Perhaps this gives him plausible deniability later on, if he happens to be humiliated by his opponent, because there are gaping holes in his argument that he didn't check before he fired it at the nearest person with a PhD or who scrapes £200 a month from selling an article. Having used such hedging and conciliatory phrases as 'I agree with you' and 'I take your point,' RebeloftheMiddle99 can thus distance himself from the original claims made – and that are under scrutiny – and make out that he agreed with his critic's views all along.

When needing a face-saving exit strategy, he will assert that the debate has gone circular so there's no point continuing. Or he will descend into misrepresentation and straw targeting in a fashion that would make an academic big cheese proud. On other occasions, RebeloftheMiddle99 will post a barrage of sources that are either palpably bogus or have nothing to do with the proposition he is making, and effectively crowd out others' contributions to a thread. I take this to be the social media equivalent of sticking one's fingers in one's ears and shouting 'la la la!' for an hour.

It's hard not to think that pathological behaviour like RebeloftheMiddle99's is enabled by the format of social media sites. When the dopamine and adrenalin are flowing, users are bound to respond to each other speedily. This can't make for careful, considered argumentation. Moreover, the literal spaces made available for you to type in your contributions to a debate are so small – I'm thinking particularly on Twitter – that nuance, balance and logical thought processes are ditched in favour of a rabble-rousing soundbite or cliché.

RebeloftheMiddle99's posts show that, from time to time, it all gets too much for him and he has a kind of breakdown. Of course, this is detailed on his accounts. I'm mentally whisked back to my being morally and emotionally blackmailed by senior managers. The vocabulary RebeloftheMiddle99 uses is so histrionic and hackneyed – 'I've hit rock bottom,' 'I don't think I can go on' – that it feels performative. The timing of these cynical attempts to court the sympathy vote – usually just after a humungous bust-up with a throng of enemies – also raises doubts about the sincerity of these sentiments. While of course people respond differently to mental distress, I know from my own experience that, when depressed, the last thing I feel like doing is to post about it every two hours on Facebook and Twitter. This is not to deny the value of catharsis, wherein a creative act articulating one's suffering with unflinching honesty can bring relief from the symptoms of that suffering. But this seems a far cry from the melodramatic platitudes RebeloftheMiddle99 is addicted to.

C shows us RebeloftheMiddle99's recent Facebook activity. I notice the profile pictures of their 'friends' and what they tell us about modern priorities. The majority are young blokes holding pints of craft lager aloft. There are also myriad young women in clubbing gear posing in lamplit city centres. Duos and trios of toddlers in fancy-dress or face-paint stand in for parents. An older woman is swimming in the sea in the middle of December. An older man roots around in his allotment. Some other older men have pics of red poppies framed by military medals.

We notice that, like millions of others, RebeloftheMiddle99 has, over time, changed his pic to stay in sync with trendy causes. First came the French flag out of sympathy with the victims of the 2015 Paris attacks, then the stars of the EU after the referendum, then, more recently, the Ukraine flag and slogans such as 'Support Iranian Women.' These pic shifts have often been accompanied by lots of fancy talk about aid, solidarity, anti-imperialism, human rights, helping refugees and the wellbeing dividends of owning an outdoor, wood-fired pizza oven.

## May 20th

Despite teaching having ended a few weeks ago, we are able to contact the suspect, whose name is R, and invite him in. Before he arrives, the AO and I scan through his academic record, which is impressive. He even won his course prize for designing an imaginative videogame-style graphical simulation of the last general election results. Reminding me of the BBC's representation of the 2004 US Presidential contest as a virtual game of American football, R's concept is a virtual game of village cricket. Symbolising the various candidates, animated batsmen dressed in red, blue, yellow and so forth would walk to the crease and perform according to how well or badly they had polled in real life. A six knocked out of the ground meant a huge swing in favour of an insurgent challenger. If a sitting MP lost their seat, then their helmeted, knee-padded avatar would be bowled, caught or out LBW.

'This sort of thing could get him hired by the BBC,' says the AO.

'Or it could cause Cotswolds colonels to melt down about an appalling waste of feepayers' money,' I reply.

Conforming to all expectations, R is entirely clad in black and has a pallid face. Part of me wants to give him a hug. Perhaps if someone had done that earlier in his life, he wouldn't have become a virtual vandal.

'Thank you for coming in to speak to us at this time when I think we'd all rather be off enjoying ourselves in the sun,' says the AO. This is a faux pas – R looks like he hides from the sun… in his mum's basement. 'A matter has arisen – a possible misconduct matter. Are you aware of the obligations that all students are under to treat others with respect?'

'I think so,' mumbles R.

'Good. When students are unhappy with any aspect of their university experience, their first port of call should be to their personal tutor. Most concerns are usually addressed at that point, so there's no need to escalate things further. However, if there is a need for escalation, the next level will be the leadership of the department.'

'I think I know what this is about,' says R. 'I didn't mean to cause offence.'

We wait for him to say more – that's all we're getting for now. I pipe up. 'What did you mean to do?'

'Make my opinion known. About how I was feeling. At the time. It's not like I used bad language or anything.'

I look over the screenshots again. 'You came quite near to it. The point is, R, your actions caused hurt and embarrassment. You must have been aware of that.'

'I don't think so. You would have to be very thin-skinned.'

The AO tries another tack. 'The other problem is the public airing you gave to your grievances. As you can understand, the university is a large organisation with a public profile and it can't tolerate misinformation being spread about it. How would you like it if someone made disparaging and untrue remarks about you to an audience of potentially millions?'

R hunches forward. Keeping his eyes down, he says, 'What public airing? Only one person would have heard what I said.'

The AO waves a sheaf of screenshots that C printed out for him. 'One person? Do you not know how social media works?'

'Social media?' gasps R.

'Yes, Facebook, Twitter, Instagram.'

'I'm not on any of those sites, they're for old people. I'm only on Discord, Parler and Rumble – and that's it. I thought all this was about that argument I had with O in her podcast production class.'

The AO turns whiter than the average host of an alt-right podcast. 'You *are* R, aren't you?'

'Yeah.'

'First name R, surname H?'

'Yeah.'

'There might be more than one student called R H,' I point out.

'No shit, Sherlock,' hisses the AO. 'R H of 128 J Avenue, Alderley Edge, Cheshire?'

'No,' says R. 'I'm from Great Yarmouth.'

I stand up and fling open the door. 'R, please accept our apologies. A case of mistaken identity. You're free to go.'

We call C and tell her of the blunder. She is understandably defensive. 'You do realise that I'm doing the jobs of three people now?'

'What are our chances of finding the R H we're after?' I ask. 'Can we now even be sure that it is any R H that we're after?'

'No,' says C. 'That was our best lead. To be honest, with the recruitment drive for next year now in full swing, I won't have the time to investigate this any further.'

'So we're stuck firefighting the phantom troll,' sighs the HoD, chucking his metaphors in a cement mixer.

# May 24th

I come into the office early to find P pacing around, hyperventilating. I ask if everything is alright.

'Not really,' he groans.

I bring him a cup of tea and ask if he wants to talk about it. He's trying to mark a batch of submissions by Chinese students who simply don't have the requisite level of English for undergraduate studies. Looking at one of the papers, I doubt it would pass muster in junior school. 'Thing is, I can't fail them,' he says.

'Well, you'll have to if they're not up to scratch.'

'No, I mean the international office has pretty much ordered me to give them all thirds.'

'Because we can't afford to let them go.'

'It'll cost us a quarter of a million quid if they walk.' P begins to dab at his eyes with a tissue. 'But worse than that, I—'

'What is it?'

'*I* taught them, so I feel like I've failed *them.*'

'It's not your fault, P. It's not the fault of any lecturer who gets landed with this shit.'

'I know it's not rational, but it's how I feel.'

This is another malaise in our sector that nobody dare speak out about. A few years ago, Murdoch University in Australia tried to sue its own maths professor Gerd Schröder-Turk for claiming on national TV that his institution admitted Chinese students who didn't have the necessary qualifications or language skills. Murdoch eventually dropped the suit, but the affair was like a warning shot to anyone else thinking of blowing the whistle anywhere else.

# June 4th

An email from the VC congratulates everyone who has been made reader and professor this year.

It doesn't take much web browsing to ascertain that, like Prof X, the bulk of these newly minted mandarins have been or are currently funded by big business and the state. One of them seems to have specialised in brokering the funding of PhD scholarships by those paragons of corporate social responsibility Monsanto, Nestle and PepsiCo. Someone else seems to have got their readership in earth sciences purely for doing consultancy work for oil-rich Arab despots.

# June 9th

Meaningless HE ritual number 3,445: our annual Grade Compliance Convention (GCC). This is a pointless, two-day-long exercise in which each unit manager reads from a report that summarises the students' grades and explains what the summer re-take task will be. There is no practical need to read this stuff out because it is all there in the report already and everyone has read it in advance of the GCC. I can only speculate that this charade makes my HoD feel special because he gets to chair it and generally boss us about.

After we each read our report out, we are questioned in a style that reminds me of being in court. 'Do you confirm that these grades are accurate?' asks my HoD of each unit manager.

'Yes, m'lud,' I'm tempted to say when it comes to my turn.

'Would you say that there were any anomalies in this year's unit?'

'No, m'lud.'

'Any additional issues you would like to make the convention aware of... before I begin sentencing?'

At the end, the various external examiners for our courses then read out reports – that we have all already read. I don't think I have ever heard any of these people say anything critical about our courses, possibly because it's a nice little earner for them and they'd like to be invited back the following year. On the contrary, they encourage us to corrode standards even further, albeit in code.

I've learned over the years that:

'You shouldn't be afraid to use the full spectrum of grades available to you' translates to 'Inflate the grades even more.'

'Offer the students a more diverse range of assessments' translates to 'don't muck about with these fuddy-duddy essays and exams, give them easy things to do like multiple choice quizzes that they can re-take as many times as they need to score 100 per cent.'

'Be more mindful of the health and wellbeing challenges students are facing' translates to 'let them have even more time to complete their assessments, meaning that, in some cases, we are still marking the previous year's work when the new academic year has begun.'

# June 15th

I get up once again ridiculously early to speak to the professor at the foreign university who will, I hope, answer my outstanding queries. What he says makes the prospective post sound less attractive. Perhaps it was always too good to be true, anyway. I start by asking what the rough time split would be between my teaching and research.

'80/20 maybe?'

'80 per cent teaching, 20 per cent research?'

'No, 80 per cent management, 20 per cent teaching. You won't have time for research initially.'

'How's that?'

'Did my colleagues not explain already?'

'No.'

'Our department is very young. For the first three or four years of your employment you would have to be essentially building the department up.'

'What does that entail?'

'Writing a new mission statement, setting up a new curriculum, hiring staff, that sort of thing.'

'Management, in other words?'

'Yes.'

Management is the one thing I have tried assiduously to avoid in my academic career, and I can't imagine it would be any less demoralising abroad. I ask him what I could spend my research budget on.

'You can use it for travel or for hiring an assistant or for equipment, should you need it. But you probably won't have time to spend it or indeed to conduct any research for those first few years.'

'First few years?'

'Yes.'

'Because I'd be too busy doing that management stuff?'

'Indeed.'

The prof then tells me that my hiring is a 'formality,' as seldom does his university's executive go against the department's decision.

Later on, while I am at lunch, I receive a call from an anonymous number. 'Hi, it's Y, one of the open day assistants. We've got applicants waiting here.'

'What's this got to do with me?'

'They're here for the open day talk about your subject.'

'They're an hour early. It's not until 1.30.'

'We have the talk as down for 12.30.'

'Ah… well, I'm at lunch.'

I abandon a jacket potato and run to the lecture theatre. Half a dozen college students and their parents are sitting in the front row, saturated with sweat. We are in the middle of a heatwave and nobody has thought to open the windows or bring in a fan. There's no air conditioning, despite this being a new building that cost a couple of million.

I try to log into the PC and projector system. My password decides to stop working. Rather than wait four hours for someone from IT to arrive, I talk without slides. The adrenaline helps me deliver a better presentation than usual, or so I tell myself.

In a small act of defiance, I don't talk about employability. Why not? Firstly, I'm sick of telling lies – there are vanishingly few graduate jobs available. Secondly, if we stop informing students that university is nothing but a stepping stone to employment, we might just prevent them from skiving and plagiarising. We might also avoid litigation, which is becoming more common.

Instead, I discuss all the other benefits – the *real* benefits, in my view – of learning and practising my subject. I'm confident because there's evidence on my side. The discipline boosts wellbeing and self-confidence. It engenders better communication – and how many conflicts micro and macro are caused by miscommunication? How often do arguments with parents or partners or siblings devolve into one side moaning that the other took something the wrong way? Learning to think critically means we are less likely to be bamboozled by politicians, advertising execs, yahoos on social media and so forth. That, in turn, makes us better citizens. So we hope.

At the end of the talk, boiling hot as we all are, a mum thanks me for my spiel. 'I've been rowing with her dad about whether O should study this subject,' she says. 'Her dad thinks it's a waste of time and money, but you've given me some new arguments I can use.'

Had our VC or even my line manager been in the room, they wouldn't have been so charitable. They may even have flung my P45 in my face. Employability is the motive power of our university today, with mammoth budgets and multiple livelihoods devoted to researching, quantifying and explicating the issue... though the ugly truth is that many more of our graduates will end up working in the local Wetherspoons than for the big names in the field.

# June 17th

I attend another university's GCC as external examiner for their MA. Lunching with the course head afterwards, it sounds like there are even worse institutions to work for than mine. She tells me that 80 per cent of her university's foreign languages lecturers have been made redundant. Now the hatchet men are going for history and English literature. Those who were union reps and most active in the recent strikes have been targeted first for dismissal.

# June 19th

As I'm marking, I spot that F, the unprepossessing conspiracist with whom I had to have a quiet word, is up to his old tricks. This time he's written a seemingly sincere and un-ironic paper about how, in the 1950s, aliens landed in a part of the USA where credulous rednecks live in igloos – and are now living and working amongst us.

Though F has gone home for the summer, he helpfully agrees to have a Zoom with me that afternoon. He's changed his image, but not for the better. He's wearing a trenchcoat, thick, goggle-like glasses and grown his hair long and straggly. He could pass for the leader of a Texan cult.

I ask him about his sources. They are all either works of fiction about alien invasion or putatively nonfiction books published by esoteric presses run by neo-Nazi chaos magicians based mostly in Montana or Somerset.

'They might be works of fiction,' F protests, 'but fiction can represent reality, like you told us in class.'

'*Can* represent, not *always* represents. F, can I just confirm that you *genuinely* believe the thesis presented in your paper?'

'Yeah, sure.'

'In that case, you can't support a truth-statement about the world with sources that are not truth-statements about the world. It would be like arguing that flying around on a broomstick is physically possible in contemporary Britain based on the Harry Potter books.'

'There's no smoke without fire. The other sources in my bibliography are people who have seen flying saucers and that.'

'They might *think* they have seen flying saucers. If something looks weird or anomalous we start by looking at the most rational explanations. Have you seen the film *Mirage Men*?'

'No.'

'Please watch it. It contains testimonies from top American spooks who, in the 1940s and '50s, fed ufologists with fake news about the little green men landing in conveniently remote parts of the Midwest.'

'Why would they do that?'

'It was to cover up something far more controversial: tests on next generation jets and missiles required for the Cold War against the USSR. These spooks reckoned it was better that the public believed there was "something out there" than to scrutinise the growing US military-industrial complex.'

F pauses in thought. 'What you've just outlined is a conspiracy theory.'

'Maybe,' I admit. 'But it's one that has more evidence going for it than the idea that' – I switch to another window on my laptop to read an excerpt from his essay. – 'Ultra-intelligent humanoids from the planet Venus are now working at the highest echelons of government, including in the Water Services Regulation Authority.'

F agrees to go away and substantially revise his essay for re-submission later.

# June 24th

The VC's end of year address. It's full of the usual excessive homilies. Nerve-racking as it is, I put my hand up at the end. I'm tempted to ask, 'How seriously do you take decolonisation when you recently accepted an honour?' But instead I pop a less facetious one on which I have spent some time working. I hope my hard graft will be rewarded with a fulsome answer.

'Over the last year the university has faced a number of challenges,' I say. 'I know we don't have time to get into the details, so I'll mention just a few examples: the flawed roll-out of our new student data system; unpopular decisions made at various levels; and failures in communication between departments and faculties that are contributing to our difficulties with recruitment, branding and marketing. Do you agree that, to some extent at least, these problems could have been solved or even avoided in the first place if there was generally more consultation, transparency and accountability – in short, democracy? Do you also agree that, as scholars in the field have proven beyond reasonable doubt, societies, communities and organisations – like universities – that are more democratic tend also to be more equal and inclusive in terms of gender, sexuality, race, ethnicity and class?'

The VC opens his mouth to answer and makes a spider with his two sets of fingertips, King Charles-style. But I'm not quite finished yet.

'It's not unusual in mainland Europe for lecturers to vote for their heads of departments and professorial chairs. The only institutions where this happens in the UK is in Oxford and Cambridge colleges. But how about introducing such measures to *our* institution?'

'Thank you, I appreciate your question,' says the VC with a pained expression that implies the complete opposite. 'These are big, big topics which we can't do justice to here. I would just say that there are already plenty of opportunities for staff at all levels – and of course students – to make their voices heard....'

The VC rattles on like this for two minutes, my attention evaporating quicker than Elon Musk's conscience after taking over a social media company.

*Consultation committees blah blah blah the two elected members of staff sit on the executive board blah blah the one non-millionaire who sits on the board of governors blah blah blah the conversations still to be had blah blah blah...*

Feeling in a more charitable mood later, I guess that, even if the VC was sympathetic to my point of view, he is limited in the reforms he can make, since the entire British HE sector arguably had all trace of democracy and egalitarianism expunged long ago.

# June 30th

I touch down somewhere in Asia at 2am, feeling more forlorn and nauseous than if I'd been forced at gunpoint to watch the complete television work of Ross Kemp. In truth, I've been on a plane for 12 hours straight and I feel this rough because (a) air travel makes me anxious, (b) I've never been able to sleep on planes and (c) the lousy food served on board is in a pitched battle with my guts. As I grip my belly and will myself not to pass out in the immigration queue, I try to remember why the hell I put myself through this. Oh yes, I'm speaking at a big conference in my academic field and the university is paying for it.

After passing under an ad hoarding for a local university that reads 'Don't you wish you had studied for a master's degree?', I get outside. It's hotter than the air that issues from Adrian Chiles' mouth. Tin roofs spread out in every direction, rough-hewn squares like a jagged chessboard. But rather than black and white, they are grey, the paint stripped off the metal by hard rain and sun. If this scene of Global Southern privation is grittily real it's also dreamlike: behind the pollution's haze these structures quiver and pall and seem only half-tangible.

I stand by a gridlock of decrepit cars and motorbikes all beeping their horns at each other, and eventually catch a taxi's attention. At numerous breaks in the journey caused by road accidents and farm animals crossing the street, hawkers bang on our windows with sponges, packs of chewing gum, cigarette cartons. On one tight corner, a gargantuan silver slab of a bus lies smashed up on its side, surrounded by yellow tape and jeeps with neon signs in their back windows reading the name of the city's police force.

'Very, very dangerous, sir,' the taxi driver says helpfully. He throws some gum into his mouth and begins weaving in and out of the wedge of traffic that has built up behind the accident. As we pass a huge open-air toilet where men squat in their dozens, the taxi driver points and declares, 'UNESCO World Heritage Site, sir!'

In a posher quarter, the stench eases off and I spot sunburned and tattooed Western kids lurking under the parasols of pavement eateries. Floral fields overgrow into the road. Less picturesque is the gated community behind the flowers, defended by high electric fencing, machine-gun nests and white-uniformed guards in pillboxes. Soon enough, the urban morphs into the rural. A freight train, sun flashing against its drawbars, slams through a milky sea of sorghum. We pass a blotchy paddy field, then a valley of tousled sugarcane, before arriving in the smaller city where the conference will be held. My hotel is in a quiet district of ragged high-rises. Washing bows from balconies, vivid colours blazing through the vehicle fumes.

I fall asleep with idle thoughts about how cities I've visited have different rhythms, like heartbeats. If the speed and intensity of this Asian city could be equated with a dangerously fast arrhythmia (the symptoms are similar too, as both a trip through this place and an attack of tachycardia can induce dizziness, the sweats and shortness of breath), then London and other Western capital cities are a healthy and athletic 150 beats per minute – and my hometown in the UK is sluggish and soporific, bordering on the brachycardic.

# June 31st

At 8am I catch a taxi to a district of the city that has been utterly globalised. It could be anywhere. I've come several thousand miles to a shopping mall containing Nike, Apple and Gucci outlets. Next door to that mall is a skyscraper so tall most of it is shrouded in clouds – or smog, I'm not sure. I take the lift to the 39th floor.

I'm greeted by a beige carpet underneath an oval-shaped wood-effect table bearing tea, coffee and pastries. Again, this could be any conference anywhere in the world. The crowd is very international. According to the descriptions on name badges, it's comprised of not just academics but businesspeople and civil servants from around Asia. I'm struck by the variable quality of the presentations. One session on the topic of traditional Egyptian dance is led by two scholars from Cairo whose English is limited. In the Q&A, an audience member asks them a simple question that engenders only confused squints and shakes of the head. The audience member simplifies their language even further, but remains misunderstood.

I feel sorry for these guys – and indignant at the conference organisers. I have my suspicions that they will accept anyone who can pay, regardless of academic credibility or ability to communicate. It may well be that the Egyptians are esteemed in their field, but they can't express themselves in English. Someone in authority should have checked this out beforehand to prevent embarrassment all round. Moreover, it's expensive enough for a Western university to send me to this shindig – I can't imagine what it costs an institution in the Global South.

The theme of global academic inequality returns at lunch. I get talking to a young, very bright female scholar from Thailand who says her PhD and other degrees from Asian universities are not taken seriously by the Western institutions she's applied to for lecturing work. She's been advised by these institutions and her mentors in Thailand to 're-train' i.e., do her degrees all over again in Western Europe, the US or Australia.

A Dutch woman, who teaches at a West African university, overhears us and confirms this. Inversely, she says, a Westerner who scraped a third-class degree in Nicolas Cage Studies at the University of Nowheresville, Nebraska or New South Wales will be able to walk into a plum job in the best academies Nepal or Nicaragua have to offer. There remains a colonial mentality, she adds, that accords prestige to Western education. Given its obeisance to the gods of mammon, I'm sure it suits Western HE to act like a closed shop. Why sabotage your own hustle of monetising foreign students by employing people with qualifications you did not yourself award?

The Thai asks me what British students are like. I gripe about poor attendance, plagiarism and the rest. When I'm done, she has been struck mute with shock.

After a while she says, 'Before I went off to study for my undergraduate degree, my father took me into his office and mapped out my future life for me on a piece of sugar paper tacked to the wall. He drew an arc and wrote things over it like "graduate with business degree age 21," "get married age 25," "own home by age 28." He told me that, from now on, I must work as hard as possible to get a good job, make money and earn respect. I would say 99 per cent of my students today are the same.'

'Those used to be Western values,' I said, thinking of the way my grandparents used to talk about education.

'Now they are world values.'

'Was your father happy that you became an academic?'

She squeezes her eyes shut and snickers. 'When I told him I had started a PhD, I thought he was going to have a stroke. He did in fact have a stroke about three years later, but I don't think it had anything to do with me saying goodbye to a *proper* career.'

After lunch I watch an older Cuban-American professor deliver a lecture that is little more than an endorsement of present US government policy towards China. 'We must build more bases in the Philippines, send more arms to Taiwan and resist Chinese aggression in the region,' he concludes. In the Q&A, I ask whether he is worried about whether this escalation will make a nuclear war more likely.

'We need to make sure *we* win before there's any risk of that,' he says.

I want to ask who *we* are and what winning might look like, but we are out of time.

# July 1st

Over morning pastries, I get talking to a Canadian lecturer who works for a university in this very city. He's a garrulous frat-boy type who tells me that his North American buddies came to visit him in the first summer he was here and that he took them out to 'get wasted' at his local bar. They took advantage of a 'bottomless brunch' deal whereby they all paid a fixed fee to drink as much as they liked for three hours. After he and his 'reprobate' friends had drained the bar of twenty beers, a bottle of whisky and a bottle of Jägermeister – and one of them had puked in the toilet – the bartender told them they were all banned. 'A group of locals would have drunk a fraction of this booze!' the Canadian cackles.

This strikes me as yet another iteration of academic colonialism – or extreme insensitivity to a culture that has welcomed and hosted you.

I deliver my own lecture to a total audience of two, neither of whom have enough English to follow me. There are no questions afterwards.

In the afternoon coffee break, I chat to the young Thai academic again. 'So do you work in London?' she asks.

'No, in a more provincial place.'

'I went to London about ten years ago.'

'How did you find it?'

'I was shocked at how *Eastern* the West was. I had no idea you read manga and watched anime, or bothered to read books by Indians and Chinese. I remember hearing that one of your politicians said that chicken tikka masala was your national dish. And then there were so many Thai restaurants in London, although not many that I wanted to eat in. But it's not just Eastern commodities you like, you are quite keen on Asian ideas and beliefs. I simply could not believe it when I saw white people doing *yoga* and *tai chi* on

Hampstead Heath, not to mention all the white Buddhists and Hare Krishnas about.'

At the end of the conference, most of the delegates decamp to a restaurant in the mall next door. I find myself sitting next to the Cuban American who lectured yesterday.

'I can tell from your accent you're British, right?' he says, as beer and pretzels are delivered to our table.

'Indeed.'

'You have great mess halls there.'

'I'm sorry?'

'The military mess halls I went to in England are classier than American ones. You always have good whisky and brandy, and the conversation is more erudite.'

'I wouldn't know. So I take it you were in the military?'

'For sure. I was in the US Army for near-on 30 years. Served in Afghanistan and Iraq. Left as a colonel.'

I determine that this is not a good time to pitch my doubts about the militarisation of HE. 'How did you get into academia?'

'Army paid for me to do my bachelor's, master's and PhD in international relations.' Now he holds a chair in war and strategic studies at a US university that sounds like it's a front business for the CIA – or at least part of its PR wing. This explains why yesterday he gave an uncritical account of American meddling in Southeast Asia. If anyone should know about the nasty consequences of American meddling in foreign countries, it ought to be someone of Cuban origin.

When we've finished our traditionally local meal of cheeseburger and chips, some other Westerners slope by our table. The colonel exchanges hugs and handshakes with them. They too work for elite institutions in the US and I quickly figure out it's for the same reasons as the colonel's meteoric rise. I'm embarrassed to tell these high-fliers my own institutional affiliation since nobody would have heard of it and, if they had, they would know it's a gulf away from Yale, Princeton and Harvard.

A preppy bloke who looks about 14 tells me he's documenting human rights abuses by the North Korean regime on a grant from the State Department and the National Endowment for Democracy. He looks Caucasian but informs me he's fluent in Korean. There's no doubting his intelligence but I wonder if someone trying to get a project off the ground exploring, say, Saudi human rights violations, would attract that level of funding and goodwill from the US government?

I get shot of the colonel and his crew, and go for a drink with some of the other delegates. The Thai woman academic is my main motivation for this. I'm already tipsy enough to pluck up the courage to ask her out for a drink tomorrow – my last and only free day of this trip – when she stands up and says her fiancée will pick her up in a few minutes.

I drown my sorrows with the others. I get into no great shape for wandering home. But I try anyway. A couple of blocks into my long and winding odyssey, I sprint across a road to avoid an oncoming scooterist, trip over the curb and smash my arm against the ground. Blood oozes out of a hole in my shirt elbow. I get back to my room, wash the wound and bandage it with some toilet paper.

# July 2nd

I find a pharmacy the next morning where I buy antiseptic, painkillers and bandages. After patching myself up, I'm still in too much agony to make use of my one free day in this city before I fly back. I lie in bed wondering if I can leave my job – and survive.

# July 3rd

Returning home, the UK feels much like the developing world I've just left. My train journey should take two hours but strikes and cancellations change the maths to five. Out the window, I watch crumbling grey polygons of cheap housing, homeless people in doorways, kids setting off firecrackers, a round-the-block queue to a food bank. At least in the developing world, students turn up to class.

# July 4th

A colleague half-jokingly asks if I 'had a nice holiday.' I am almost ready to punch their teeth down their throat.

# July 6th

I mark the re-submission work handed in by students who failed or missed their deadlines the first time round. F the conspiracist has submitted something even more deranged than the 'aliens are living amongst us' shtick I had to tell him off about last month. He's missed my point about irrational conspiracy theories being promoted to conceal more controversial goings-on. His new draft is so inventively weird that I might give him a first if this were a creative writing unit. I can't, though, as this unit requires students to write factually about the real world.

F speculates that a well-known actor's PR team were spreading rumours that he was attending orgies, having sex with random women and other Jack-the-lad stuff, in order to cover up that he is gay. I search for stories online to back this up. The actor in question has the Lothario rep, but there's no evidence that he's closeted. The first comment I write down for F is: 'Don't publish this anywhere or you'll be done for libel.'

Stranger still, F's essay goes on to discuss a provincial politician in the American Midwest who was being harassed by hard-right Trump supporters for, in their diseased minds, being a member of the reptilian overclass. They'd trolled him online, followed his wife and kids in their pick-up trucks, and stood outside city hall barking accusations through megaphones about pizza and paedophilia. F's theory is that this politician's spin doctors came up with this cunning plan. When the politician went out for his morning jog he'd wear a T-shirt with that all-seeing-eye-on-a-pyramid picture on it that's supposed to be the official logo of the Illuminati. Then, in a press conference, he told a folksy, down-home proverb about catching a lizard. Then, alleges F, one of his staff went onto some neo-Nazi website and wrote an article alleging that the politician's forefathers back in Europe had not only financed the Russian Revolution but were somehow complicit in the July 1944 plot to assassinate Hitler.

F's thesis is that the politician's spin doctors actively fuelled this conspiracy in order to distract from the far murkier truth of what was going on behind the scenes: the politician and his cronies were embezzling millions of dollars from local construction contracts and property deals.

I try to verify these details. I can only locate articles exposing this politician for the fraud that F mentions. There is nothing out there about him being tormented by cranks, or his team fanning the flames of conspiracy theories about him. Seemingly F has fabricated this entire dimension of the story.

I email him asking for an urgent meeting.

# July 10th

A few days have passed and there is no reply from F. I email the admin responsible for the course he's on and am informed that F has withdrawn from the university. Perhaps he has been whisked to a secret New World Order death camp on Mars.

# July 11th

I finally hear back from a major funding body about a bid I submitted for a research project some months ago. It is rated 'very good,' though that's not enough for them to pay up, which is tantalising and infuriating. Reading the feedback, I speculate whether there's been a mix-up somewhere, because the comments seemingly relate to a totally different project. One of the peer reviewer's reports is jam-packed with solecisms such as 'There is no mention of or supporting information about the financial support to be provided by the institution.' However, there are several pages in my online application explaining just that. It appears that almost any old buffoon can get to be a peer reviewer, since the other report is full of spelling errors. Once again, the sloppiness stems from the lack of resourcing. The treadmill of production that is modern academic research involves masses of journals and other organisations all competing to churn out material and survive in a shark-infested market... so it's no wonder that anyone who will work for free and can spell their own name – while not necessarily being able to spell other words – could be drafted in. I recall that no sooner had I embarked on a PhD and obtained some adjunct hours for about the same remuneration as a Deliveroo cyclist, I was receiving invites to review this bid or that journal paper. Only occasionally would these documents align with my actual expertise.

These journals and funding bodies would ideally recruit people who know what they are doing, but the hitch here is that many competent, full-time academics are so busy being competent, full-time academics they don't have the time.

I notice in one of the reports received for this current bid a diktat to cite the work of a well-known academic in the field. Although the writer of the report is anonymous, I suspect that they are in fact this very academic. This is not unusual. Since they aren't getting paid for this task, they may as well get a citation out of it.

This naughty practice is replicated in teaching. As an undergrad, I had a lecturer who was possibly the greatest dullard who ever lived and he filled our reading list with his own books and articles. I have colleagues today who do the same, in the teeth of student feedback along the lines of, 'I felt pressured to buy so-and-so's book.' Any peer reviewer worth a damn should try to see things from the author's perspective and offer advice to help them deliver *their* vision.

I've already bored you with the observation that universities aren't democracies. Funding bodies don't seem to be either, for the brusque email informing me of the peer reviewers' decision reads at the bottom, 'this is final' – a phrase menacingly redolent of kidnappers about to send a severed thumb 'cuz the braahn envelope ain't arrived!'

# July 15th

I receive a curt email from the foreign university: We regret to inform you that we will not be offering you the role. After great deliberation we believe that you would struggle to adapt to our culture and society. Furthermore, your research interests do not quite align with the institution's agenda.

While I almost certainly wouldn't have accepted the offer anyway, I find myself unexpectedly furious about this outcome. Could you give me some more feedback? I reply. What you have furnished me with so far is pathetically brief and makes no sense. I've worked abroad before and would have no trouble working abroad again. Over these last few months, your staff have repeatedly informed me that my research interests would align with your institution's agenda, so why the sudden change of mind? I was told only a few weeks ago that my offer would be a 'formality.'

## July 16th

I receive an email from one of the people who interviewed me for the foreign university job. They say they will try to obtain further feedback for me.

## July 28th

It has been almost two weeks since I was told I'd get further feedback on the foreign job and none has been received. I email my contact and ask him how I can make a complaint to his institution.

He emails me back quickly. I feel you are harassing me now. I understand that you are upset about being rejected by our institution, but this is all the information we can give you.

I'm not upset about being rejected, I reply. I almost certainly wouldn't have accepted the offer anyway. But that's not the point. The point is, it is highly unprofessional to waste someone's time like this, compelling them to attend many meetings and deliver a long presentation, only to furnish them with vague and nonsensical feedback. Any serious institution of learning should be accountable for its decisions.

# July 29th

In his next email my contact threatens to report me to my institution if I keep 'harassing' him. This strikes me as blackmail and makes me wonder if I dodged a bullet by not transferring to an institution that is even more morally defective than my current employer.

I leave it there. It's not worth the blood pressure. Instead, I email the international job website where I found the advert for the gig and warn them about this institution's unethical ways.

# August 30th

With the new academic year looming, colleagues are worried that management have not yet revoked J's promotion to course chief. The fear is that the HoD is too cowardly to confront J and/or not smart enough to solve this thorny problem. The plaintiffs have tried to assist by positing some solutions themselves. How about getting J to make certain commitments to *not* being an unprofessional tit once he takes up the post? The HoD has fudged this by claiming that he's confident J will 'step up to the plate.' One plaintiff, though, doubts this could happen given all of J's psychological flaws. In an act of irresponsible deflection, the HoD has warned that J could launch a counter-grievance of bullying against what he – and the powers that be – might perceive as a vindictive conspiracy against him.

# 31st August

Sick of the HoD stalling, the plaintiffs have taken the nuclear option. Having consulted with a union rep who told them that they shouldn't have to work with or for someone who has bullied them, the four higher-ranked plaintiffs have demanded that J be denied promotion – or else they won't teach on his course. Should J take office, the lower-ranking plaintiffs have said they will all launch formal grievances against him.

# 3rd September

My spies tell me that the HoD has backed down and will not promote J. Though democratic accountability is in short supply in the modern academy, a livid, quasi-blackmail-driven revolt can change a manager's mind – especially if it means extra work and a reputation left in tatters by HR investigations and employment tribunals. My feeling about this is the same as my feeling about almost every conflict in HE – why is it always allowed to reach a crescendo of stress and recrimination, when an amicable resolution could have been reached months ago?

# 9th September

With the students having just arrived for the new year, I host an evening of talks by them and certain colleagues involved in a journal I helped set up. W, a female student, overcomes her anxiety to read an article she has written for the occasion. I feel incredibly proud of her. At the end, an elderly working-class couple come up to me. The man says, 'We're W's grandparents. We've never been to anything like this before and we just wanted to say what a fabulous time we've had tonight.' For a moment all my travails melt into the air. This is worth more than receiving a good performance review from my HoD or winning an award for *outreach* or *knowledge transfer*.

# Epilogue

Reading this book may have lowered your opinion of the entire British university system. While there *is* valid cause for despair, my account probably accentuates the negative aspects of my job. The events above demonstrating mendacity, incompetence and bigotry greatly outnumber the incidents of joy and success in teaching and research. In reality, across my career there have been many bright moments that I have not mentioned in this book. This doesn't mean I have set out to be deliberately gloomy. All writing based on real life involves selecting and excluding material, and I have definitely leant towards the material that demonstrates the mess HE is in. My idealistic aim is that someone, somewhere might read this book and be cheesed off enough to clear up the mess.

I want to now suggest what could be done to help universities pull back from the intellectual, moral, ideological and administrative precipice they are staring dumbly into. We should start by questioning the canard that corporatisation drives up standards and makes things better. You don't need to have been anywhere near a university, let alone have a PhD in economics, to know that competition is just as likely to engender deceit, inefficiency and corner-cutting.

We could mitigate the mania for markets in HE by abolishing tuition fees, a popular, costed policy of the Labour Party in the 2017 and 2019 elections. In addition to saving future generations from baleful debt, this could fix the damage done by the 'gimme gimme gimme' customer mentality that now dominates the sector.

If the corporate model of HE is here to stay – sadly, it looks that way – institutions should at least start using their resources more wisely. The gigantic and pointless managerial armies of darkness – VCs, deans, vice deans, deputy deans, heads of this, heads of that etc – could be culled and the money spent instead on those neglected functions that are so much more important for any organisation that can plausibly call itself a university: teaching, research, mentoring, health and wellbeing.

If HE mandarins were to start sincerely giving a toss about their underlings' welfare, they would bring in policies to ban overwork, zero hours contracts and non-disclosure agreements about bullying and harassment. Even better would be for government to pass laws doing so.

Universities must stop thinking in the abstract about politics, ethics and morality. Equality, diversity and decolonisation should not be mere PR gimmicks used to fish money out of the pockets of progressive-minded potential students while, behind the scenes, universities collaborate with authoritarian, murderous and ecocidal outfits. If we're serious about ethics, let's divest from repressive state apparatuses, arms dealers and fossil fuel companies. This procedure should start with an honest reckoning with the 'political economy' of universities, how they function in the world today and how they have in the past. A valuable trailblazer here has been Cambridge University historian Priyamvada Gopal, whose campaign resulted in her institution investigating its historic complicity in the Atlantic slave trade. Crucially, the campaign directly linked that previous atrocity to contemporary forms of racial violence, unlike institutions with less integrity who have performatively critiqued the imperial past while failing to acknowledge present-day neo-imperial power, for which they must share some of the blame.

Finally, there must be a realisation that all the problems sketched out above – the solutions to which are words beginning with 'd' – decarbonisation, demilitarisation, decolonisation etc – are connected and should be alleviated with more of another 'd': democracy. The sharpest of campus novelists, David Lodge, wrote in *Ginger You're Barmy*, his semi-autobiographical account of doing national service in the 1950s, 'The Army... was the last surviving relic of feudalism in English society.' The same can be said of universities 70 years later. If we get to vote for our MPs, councillors, union leaders and even for our favourite singer-who-can't-really-sing on telly, why can't we vote for the person we are answerable to at work? At least if a workforce ends up electing the wrong person for the job, they can only blame themselves and not some arcane, Freemasonic-style deal struck behind closed doors by a handful of bigwigs completely remote from the 'shop floor.'

The often astringent criticisms in this book are not intended as an attack on the very point or existence of universities. On the contrary, universities are vital to a society that aspires to knowledge, freedom and democracy. It's just that universities have lost sight of what being a university means. Can that change? I really really hope so.

# Sources[1]

- Al Jazeera Investigative Unit, 'Documents reveal discrimination and racism in UK Labour Party,' *Al Jazeera*, 29th September 2022.
- Miles Allen-Rhond, 'Right-thinking Academics,' *Morning Star*, 2023.
- Kingsley Amis, *Lucky Jim, London and* New York, Penguin Classics, 2000.
- Kehinde Andrews, *The New Age of Empire: How Racism and Colonialism Still Rule the World*, London and New York, Penguin, 2021.
- AOAV, 'The £1bn deals between the UK universities and the arms trade reviewed,' *Action on Armed Violence*, 14th February 2023.
- David Batty, 'Birmingham University warned of risk to LGBT rights at Dubai campus,' *Guardian*, 14th November 2018.

---

[1] Just so you can be reassured that I haven't made all the stuff up in this book, here are links to where I acquired the information about people and events I don't have lived experience of.

- Maggie Berg and Barbara Karolina Seeber, *The Slow Professor: Challenging the Culture of Speed in the Academy*, Toronto, University of Toronto Press, 2016.
- Malcolm Bradbury, *The History Man*, London, Picador, 2017.
- Billy Briggs, 'US Christian right "dark money" backed anti-abortion Glasgow students,' the ferret.scot, 28th March 2019.
- Ben Burgess, *Canceling Comedians While the World Burns: A Critique of the Contemporary Left*, London and New York, Zero Books, 2021.
- 'Chinese money is pouring into British universities,' Economist.com, 12th March 2022.
- Catherine Chiniara Charrett, 'How a Palestinian academic defeated a campaign to silence her,' *Al Jazeera*, 10th February 2022.
- Noam Chomsky and Edward S. Herman, *Manufacturing Consent: The Political Economy of the Mass Media*, New York, Pantheon Books, 1988.
- Stefan Collini, *What Are Universities For?*, London, Penguin UK, 2012.
- Raewynn Connell, *The Good University: What Universities Actually Do and Why It's Time for Radical Change*, London, Zed Books, 2019.
- Jenna Corderoy, 'British universities slammed for taking £90m from oil companies in four years,' *Open Democracy*, 11th December 2021.
- Jonathan Dean, 'Political Science in the Age of the Pol Prof,' *New Socialist*, 9th July 2021.

- Lizzie Dearden, 'UK "complicit in killing civilians and risks being prosecuted over illegal drone operations", major report suggests,' *Independent*, 17th July 2018.
- Terry Eagleton, 'The slow death of the university,' *The Chronicle of Higher Education*, 21st April 2015.
- John Ehrenreich and Barbara Ehrenreich, 'The new left and the professional-managerial class,' *Radical America*, 11 (3), 1977.
- Equality and Human Rights Commission, *Tackling Racial Harassment: Universities Challenged*, 2020.
- Mark Erickson, Paul Hanna & Carl Walker, 'The UK higher education senior management survey: a statactivist response to managerialist governance,' *Studies in Higher Education*, 46:11, 2021.
- Dan Evans, *A Nation of Shopkeepers: The Unstoppable Rise of the Petite Bourgeoisie*, London, Repeater Books, 2023.
- Hannah Ewens, 'How more than 12 students at one university ended up dead by suicide,' *VICE*, 8th October, 2019.
- 'Facebook founder warns of social media addiction,' *ABC News*, 10th November 2017.
- Frantz Fanon, *The Wretched of the Earth*, London and New York, Penguin Classics, 2001.
- Frantz Fanon, *Black Skin, White Masks*, London and New York, Penguin Classics, 2021.
- Guy Faulconbridge, 'Ukraine war already with up to 354,000 casualties, likely to last past 2023 – U.S. documents,' *Reuters*, 12th April 2023.

- Anna Fazackerley, '"Despicable in a pandemic": fury as UK universities plan job cuts,' *Guardian*, 22nd January 2021.
- Mark Fisher, *Capitalist Realism: Is There No Alternative?*, London and New York, Zero Books, 2012.
- Peter Fleming, *How Universities Die*, London, Pluto Press, 2021.
- Mariko L. Frame, 'Ecological imperialism: A world-systems approach,' *Am J Econ Sociol*, 81, 2022.
- Ian Freckleton, 'Research fraud: the temptation to lie – and the challenges of regulation,' *The Conversation*, 5th July 2016.
- Marcus Gilroy-Ware, *Filling the Void: Emotion, Capitalism & Social Media*, London, Repeater Books, 2017.
- Marcus Gilroy-Ware, *After the Fact: The Truth About Fake News*, London, Repeater Books, 2020.
- Hannah Graham, 'Newcastle University now has its own campus cat – and students are already in love with her,' chroniclelive.co.uk, 10th June 2022.
- Jack Grove, 'UCU: sexual harassment rife as UK universities "protect predators",' *Times Higher Education*, 22nd December 2021.
- House of Commons Library, *Student Loan Statistics*, 2023.
- Dominic Kennedy, 'Conspiracy theories spread by academics with university help,' *The Times*, 13th June 2020.

- Christopher Ketcham, 'The troubling case of Chris Hedges,' *The New Republic*, 12th June 2014.
- Christopher Knaus, 'Murdoch University sues whistleblower after comments on international students,' Guardian.com, 11th October 2019.
- Christopher Knaus, 'Murdoch University drops plans to sue whistleblower over student exploitation comments,' Guardian.com, 14th January 2020.
- Trymaine Lee, 'Black Lives Matter releases policy sgenda,' *NBC News*, August 1st 2016.
- Catherine Liu, *Virtue Hoarders: The Case against the Professional Managerial Class*, Minneapolis, MN, University of Minnesota Press, 2021.
- David Lodge, *Changing Places*, London and New York, Vintage, 2011.
- David Lodge, *Ginger You're Barmy*, London and New York, Vintage, 2011.
- David Lodge, *Nice Work*, London and New York, Vintage, 2011.
- David Lodge, *Small World*, London and New York, Vintage, 2011.
- Lundberg, John, Roland Denning, and Kypros Kyprianou. 'Mirage Men,' 2013. based on a script by Mark Pilkington, with contributions from Paul Bennewitz (archive), Greg Bishop, Walter Bosley, Stephen Broadbent, James Carrion, Richard M. Dolan, Robert Emenegger, Peter Gersten, Dr. Christopher Green, Richard C. Doty, Robert Durant, George Hansen, Linda Moulton Howe, Victor Martinez,

William Moore (archive), Curtis Peebles, Mark Pilkington, Ron Regehr, Bill Ryan, and Gabe Valdez.

- Bruce Macfarlane, 'The neoliberal academic: Illustrating shifting academic norms in an age of hyper-performativity,' *Educational Philosophy and Theory*, 53, 2021.
- Basit Mahmood, 'Muslim woman told to "go home" by Oxford University worker,' *Metro*, 30th September 2019.
- Todd McGowan, *The Racist Fantasy: Unconscious Roots of Hatred*, London and New York, Bloomsbury Academic, 2022.
- Arron Merat, '"The Saudis couldn't do it without us": the UK's true role in Yemen's deadly war,' *Guardian*, 18th June 2019.
- Ben van den Merwe, 'Right-wing dark money comes to Oxford student politics,' *Cherwell*, 28th January 2019.
- Jack Mirkinson and Rebecca Shapiro, 'Fareed Zakaria suspended for plagiarism: Time Editor, CNN Host apologizes for "terrible mistake",' Huffpost.com, 10th October 2012.
- Sinéad Murphy, *Zombie University: Thinking Under Control*, Watkins Media Limited, 2017.
- Maddy Mussen, 'President of the United States and king of gaffes: The best and worst lines from Joe Biden,' *Evening Standard*, 26th April 2023.
- John Henry Newman, *The Idea of a University: Defined and Illustrated*, independently published, 2021.

- David Nicholls, *Starter for Ten*, London, Hodder Paperbacks, 2004.
- Annie Nova and Nate Rattner, 'College graduates owe $29,000 in student debt now – more than ever before,' cnbc.com, 19th September 2019.
- Office for National Statistics, *Estimating Suicide Among Higher Education Students, England and Wales: Experimental Statistics: 2017 to 2020,* 2021.
- The Plymouth Institute for Peace Research, 'University of Plymouth leaked emails expose staff abuse,' 17th March 2023.
- Claire Provost, 'Revealed: US anti-LGBT "hate group" dramatically increases UK spending,' openDemocracy. net, 20th March 2019.
- David Richardson, cited in Linda Adey, 'Is Uni Racist? Black and ethnic minority students allege mishandling of racism complaints,' bbc.co.uk, 5th May 2021.
- Richard Seymour, *The Twittering Machine: How Capitalism Stole Our Social Life*, London, Repeater Books, 2019.
- Samira Shackle, '"The way universities are run is making us ill": inside the student mental health crisis,' guardian.com, 27th September 2019.
- Hazel Shearing and Lucy Gilder, Student finance: How much does university cost and does it increase earnings?,' *BBC News*, 31st August 2023.
- Charlotte Smith, 'Almost half of students do not think that university is worth the money,' coventrylive.com, 6th September 2023.

- Zadie Smith, *On Beauty,* London and New York, Penguin, 2006.
- John Smyth, *The Toxic University: Zombie Leadership, Academic Rock Stars and Neoliberal Ideology,* London and New York, Palgrave, 2018.
- Steerpike, 'Bristol refuse to declare Miller probe costs,' *Spectator,* 6th January 2022.
- 'Stop Islamophobia at Bristol University: #ScraptheModule,' Change.org, 27th January 2021.
- Matthew Taylor and Jeevan Vasagar, 'Student protests: police ask colleges for student details,' *Guardian,* 17th January 2011.
- Thompson, E.P., *Warwick University Ltd: Industry, Management and the Universities,* London, Spokesman Books, 2013.
- Igea Troiani and Claudia Dutson, 'The neoliberal university as a space to learn/think/work in higher education,' *Architecture and Culture,* 9 (1), 2021.
- Kieron Turner, 'Disrupting coloniality through Palestine solidarity: Decolonising or decolonial praxis?,' *Interfere,* 3, 2022.
- UCU, *Precarious Work in Higher Education,* 2021.
- UCU, 'New analysis reveals record university income as employers refuse to negotiate,' 17th May 2023.
- '"Under pressure" Cardiff University lecturer fell to death,' *BBC News,* 6th June 2018.
- Amy Varley, 'Student left "suicidal" after Sheffield hired private investigator to look into occupations,' *Sheffield Tab,* 4th April 2023.

- Paolo Virno, 'The ambivalence of disenchantment,' in Paolo Virno and Michael Hardt (eds.), *Radical Thought in Italy,* Minneapolis, MN, University of Minnesota Press, 2006.
- John B. Warren, 'The trouble with antidepressants: Why the evidence overplays benefits and underplays risks,' *BMJ*, 2020; 370, 2020.
- Evelyn Waugh, *Brideshead Revisited,* London, Chapman and Hall, 1964.
- Jacob Weisberg, 'W.'s greatest hits,' Slate.com, 12th January 2009.
- World Health Organization, 'Mental health at work,' 28th September 2022.
- Chris Yorke and Ewan Somerville, 'Professor Piers Robinson leaves Sheffield Uni post after accusations of promoting conspiracy theories,' *Huffington Post,* 13th May 2019.
- Toby Young, 'David Miller may be a loon, but sacking him would open a Pandora's Box,' *The Critic,* 25th February 2021.
- Shoshana Zuboff, *Surveillance Capitalism: The Fight for a Human Future at the New Frontier of Power,* London: Profile Books, 2018.

# Index

# More titles from Canbury Press

How to Apologise for Killing a Cat
Rhetoric and the Art of Persuasion
Guy Doza
Rhetoric

'Most books on persuasion teach the few how to sway the many. With wit and vim, Guy has given us something else: an X-ray into the tactics of those trying to change our minds and behaviour.'
**Stephen Krupin, former speechwriter for Barack Obama**

# More titles from Canbury Press

Missing the Mark
Why So Many School Exam Grades are Wrong – and
How to Get Results We Can Trust
Dennis Sherwood
Education

'Everyone in UK education should reflect upon the
problems identified in this powerful book'
**Higher Education Policy Institute**